with CD

Helen Marlais'
Succeeding at the Piano™
A Method for Everyone
Let's Play!

WHAT YOU NEED

A piano

The desire to learn

Time to practice

Your imagination!

COMPOSERS

Timothy Brown

Kevin Costley

Mary Leaf

Helen Marlais

Kevin Olson

ISBN-13: 978-1-56939-844-9

Production: Frank J. Hackinson
Production Coordinators: Joyce Loke, Satish Bhakta, and Philip Groeber
Editors: Joyce Loke, Edwin McLean, Peggy Gallagher, and Nancy Bona-Baker
Art Direction: Sandy Brandvold and Andi Whitmer – in collaboration with Helen Marlais
Cover and Interior Illustrations: ©2010 Susan Hellard/Arena
Cover and Interior Illustration Concepts: Helen Marlais
Engraving: Tempo Music Press, Inc.
Printer: Tempo Music Press, Inc.

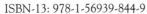

THE
F·J·H
MUSIC
COMPANY
INC.
Frank J. Hackinson

Table of Contents

Technique is found on pages 4, 5, 10, 11, 14, 18, 20, 30, 38, 46, 49, 60, 66, 67, 71, and 77.

It is impossible to know when music began. People have been playing musical instruments for thousands of years!

Playing the piano is something very special because you can make music on your own!

Throughout your lessons, you will learn about many famous composers who wrote beautiful music. One of the most famous composers of all time, Franz Joseph Haydn, will be your first guide in this method. He was called "Papa" Haydn, because everyone who knew him loved and respected him. He helped many musicians throughout his lifetime and was a wonderful teacher. Papa Haydn will help you listen, learn, and play!

Papa Haydn lived from 1732-1809, and his birthday was March 31. He spent most of his life living and working in a palace!

(Haydn is pronounced "HI - din")

Technique with Papa Haydn

At the Piano

1. With your hands on your lap, sit comfortably on the bench, in the "middle" of the piano. (Your teacher will help you.) If your feet can't reach the floor, place a stool or a piece of wood under them.

2. Sit towards the front half of the bench with your body weight evenly distributed between your feet and the seat. Your forearms and wrists should be parallel to the floor. If they are not, place a few books on the bench and sit on them.

3. **Ask yourself:**

- Am I sitting tall?

- Are my wrists at the same level as my forearms?

- Are my elbows at the same level or slightly above the top of the white keys on the piano?

- Can I shift my weight from hip to hip (left to right)?

- Are my knees under the piano?

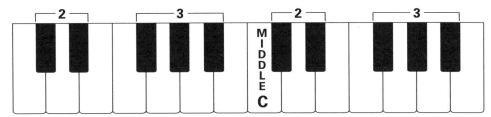

This is the keyboard. It has white and black keys. There are groups of 2 and 3 black keys on the piano.

Your teacher will help you find and play the black keys and Middle C.

REVIEW THIS PAGE OFTEN. PLACE A ✔ UNDER EACH DAY YOU DO IT.

MONDAY	TUESDAY	WEDNESDAY	THURSDAY	FRIDAY	SATURDAY	SUNDAY
___	___	___	___	___	___	___

FJH2051

Technique with Papa Haydn
Learning a natural hand position

1. Hand position is very important. It is the first step in making a beautiful sound.

  • People play the piano all over the world! Look at Papa Haydn and the piano student as they place their hands over the globes.

"Perfect Piano Hands"

L.H.
(Left hand)

R.H.
(Right hand)

2. Imagine that your hand is covering the top of the little globe. Now form your own rounded, natural hand position for playing.

  • Look at your hands—do you notice your curved fingers?
  • Do you notice the space between your fingers?
  • Do you notice how your knuckles look?

PLACE A ✓ UNDER THE DAYS YOU DID THIS PAGE.

MONDAY	TUESDAY	WEDNESDAY	THURSDAY	FRIDAY	SATURDAY	SUNDAY
___	___	___	___	___	___	___

The Steady Beat

 Rhythm marks time in music.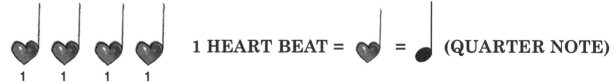

1 HEART BEAT = ♩ = ♩ (QUARTER NOTE)

With your teacher,

1. Stand in place and clap this beat:

2. Stand and lightly tap your head with your hands to every beat.

3. Walk around the room and swing your arms back and forth with every beat.

4. Sit on the piano bench and sway to the beat.

Which picture shows you a steady beat? Circle it!

Two Black Keys

Before playing:

- Raise the hand that will start.
- Wiggle the fingers you will use.
- Gently press these fingers in your lap.
- Tap and count aloud.

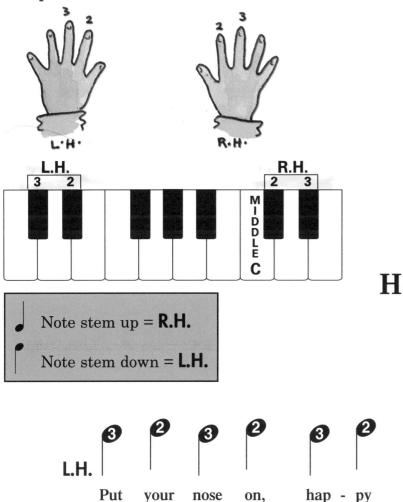

♩ Note stem up = **R.H.**

♩ Note stem down = **L.H.**

Happy Clown
by Helen Marlais

CD 2 • MIDI 1

Lift your hands off the keys, *wrists first*, and place them on your lap.

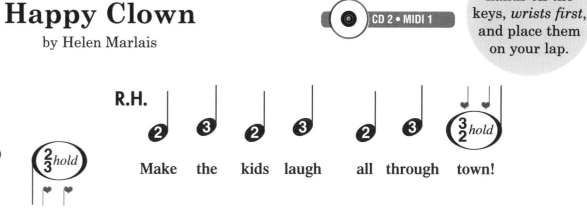

R.H.

2   3   2   3   2   3   ³⁄₂ *hold*

Make   the   kids   laugh   all   through   town!

L.H.

3   2   3   2   3   2   ²⁄₃ *hold*

Put   your   nose   on,   hap - py   clown!

(When students play this piece slowly, they can achieve a feeling of arm weight by dropping into each note playing *non-legato*.
Have students count aloud first and then say the words in rhythm, holding the last note of each group twice as long as the others.
For example: 1 1 1 1 1 1 1 2   ♩ = 1 beat; ♩ = 2 beats)

Before playing:

- Circle the hand that will begin this piece.

- There are 2 groups of notes in the piece.
  Which hand begins the 2nd group? _____

- Tap and count aloud. Each "big" note gets 2 heartbeats.

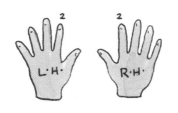

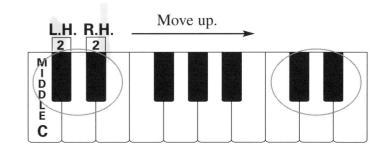

Move up.

L.H. R.H.

CD 3 • MIDI 2

Monkeys Up in the Trees
by Helen Marlais

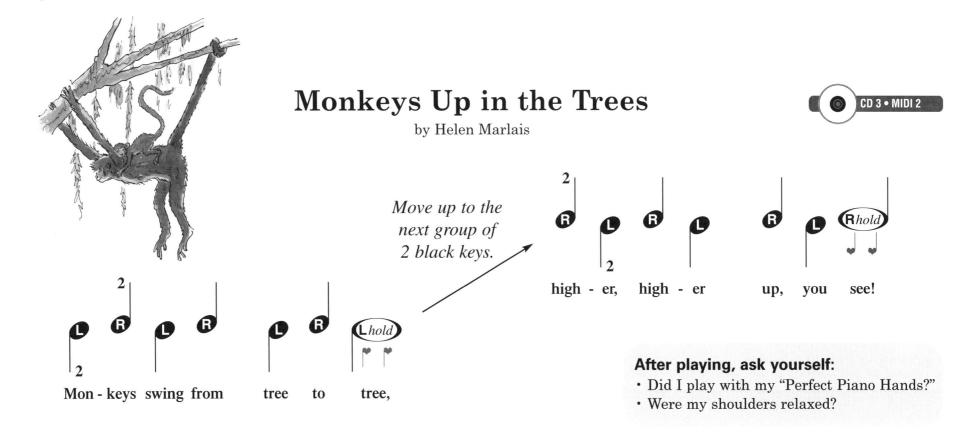

Move up to the next group of 2 black keys.

2
R L R L R L Rhold

high - er, high - er up, you see!

L R L R L R Lhold

Mon - keys swing from tree to tree,

After playing, ask yourself:
- Did I play with my "Perfect Piano Hands?"
- Were my shoulders relaxed?

DUET PART: Kevin Olson (student plays as written)

(Encourage students to play with their hands, wrists, and forearms moving as one unit.)

Before playing:

- Circle the hand that will begin this piece.

- Which hand begins the 2nd group? _____

- Tap and say the words. Hold the last note of each group twice as long as the others.

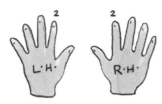

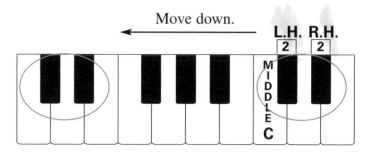

Move down.

Monkeys Back on the Ground

by Helen Marlais

CD 4 • MIDI 3

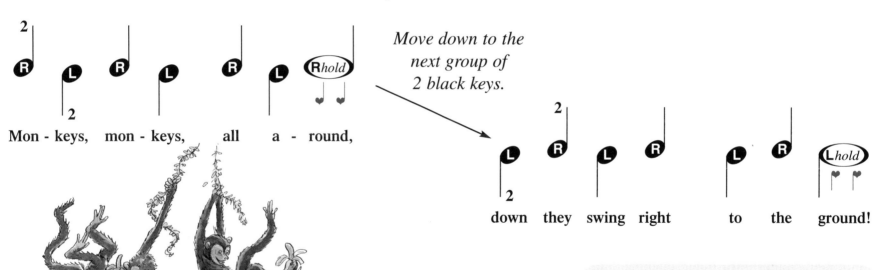

Move down to the next group of 2 black keys.

Mon - keys, mon - keys, all a - round,

down they swing right to the ground!

After playing, ask yourself:

- How are *Monkeys Up in the Trees* and *Monkeys Back on the Ground* different?

DUET PART: Kevin Olson (student plays 1 octave higher)

"Warm-ups for the Body" with Papa Haydn

Learning finger numbers

1. Every finger has a number:

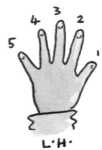
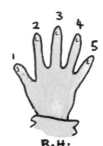

(Left hand)   (Right hand)

- Raise your L.H. in the air in front of you.
  Wiggle your thumb, or your "1" finger!
  Wiggle your pointer finger, or your "2" finger!
  Wiggle your "3" finger!
  Wiggle your "4" finger!
  Wiggle your "5" finger!

- Raise your R.H. in the air in front of you.
  Wiggle your thumb, or your "1" finger!
  Wiggle your pointer finger, or your "2" finger!
  Wiggle your "3" finger!
  Wiggle your "4" finger!
  Wiggle your "5" finger!

2. How fast can you do this?
Touch your "1" fingers together in the air.
Touch your "3" fingers together in the air.
Touch your "5" fingers together in the air.
Touch your "2" fingers together in the air.
Touch your "4" fingers together in the air.

                                                  FJH2051

Learning posture and arm weight

Posture

- Stand tall, with your arms relaxed.
- Scrunch up your shoulders—can they reach your ears? Now drop your shoulders and relax your arms.
- Do this twice.
- Play the piano with your shoulders relaxed.

Arm weight

- Imagine your arms are sandbags.
- Move your arms straight in front of you and reach forward! Then drop your arms to the sides and feel like they are sandbags again.
- This relaxed feeling of arm weight is important.

REVIEW PAGES 4, 5, 10, AND 11 OFTEN. PLACE A ✔ UNDER EACH DAY YOU DO IT.

MONDAY	TUESDAY	WEDNESDAY	THURSDAY	FRIDAY	SATURDAY	SUNDAY
___	___	___	___	___	___	___

Three Black Keys

Circle the groups of 3 black keys below.

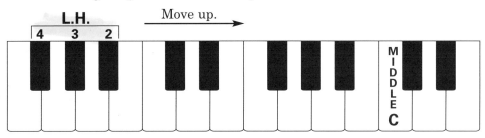

Before playing:

- Form your L.H. "Perfect Piano Hand."
- Prepare the 1st black-key group. Then **look** to the next **higher** group of 3 black keys. When you are ready to move to this next group, do so smoothly. Practice this move many times before you begin this piece so you know where you are going!
- Tap and count aloud. Each "big" note gets 3 heartbeats.

double bar line
(The piece has ended.)

CD 5 • MIDI 4

Zebras and Skunks

by Helen Marlais

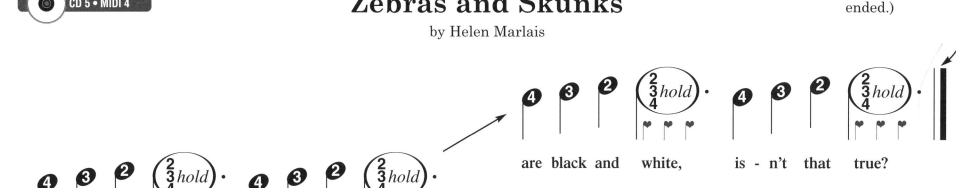

Ze - bras and skunks, pia - no keys too,

are black and white, is - n't that true?

For teacher use:

(♩ = 1 beat; ♩. = 3 beats)

After playing, ask yourself:
- Did I play with rounded and strong fingers?
- Did I move smoothly?

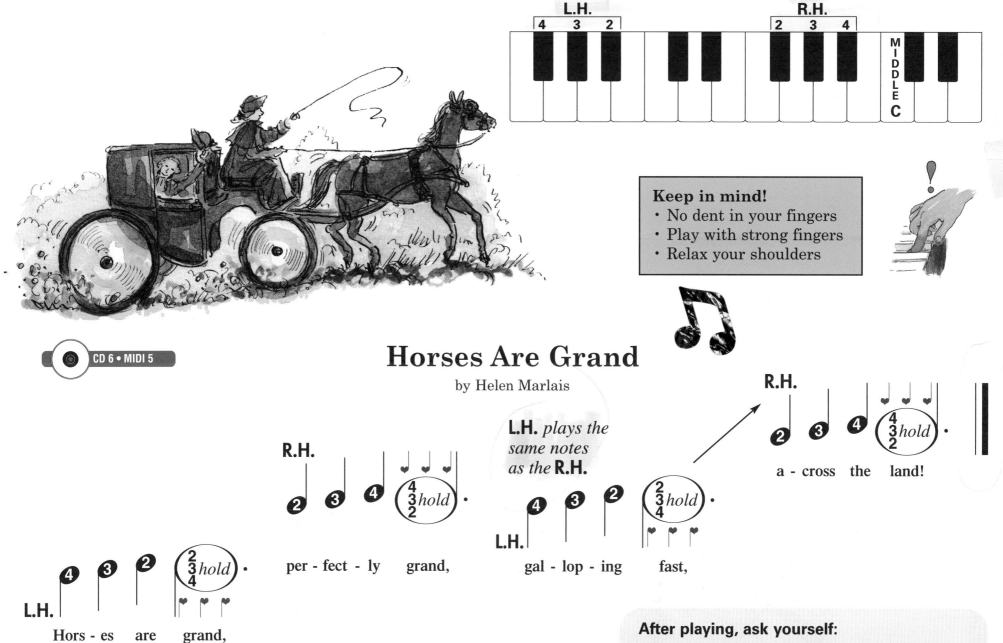

Keep in mind!
- No dent in your fingers
- Play with strong fingers
- Relax your shoulders

CD 6 • MIDI 5

Horses Are Grand

by Helen Marlais

L.H. plays the same notes as the R.H.

R.H.

R.H.

L.H.

L.H.

Hors - es   are   grand,

per - fect - ly   grand,

gal - lop - ing   fast,

a - cross   the   land!

After playing, ask yourself:
- Did I play with "Perfect Piano Hands?"
- Did I play with a steady beat?
- Did I let my wrist lift at the end of each group?

Technique with Papa Haydn

Reviewing "Perfect Piano Hands"

1. This is the natural, rounded hand position you need when you are playing the piano.

2. Imagine a ping pong ball underneath your hand. Look at the rounded shape.

3. Can you see an oval shape between your thumb and index finger? Try not to have "fly-away" fingers!

4. Draw a smiley face next to the **outside tip** of your thumbnails. This is the spot where you should play when playing with your thumbs.

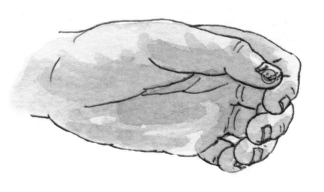

FJH2051

The White Keys

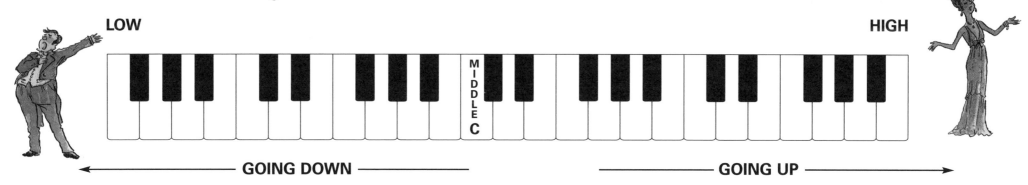

LOW   HIGH

MIDDLE C

◄———— GOING DOWN ————————   ———————— GOING UP ————►

1. The white keys on the keyboard have letter names which use the first 7 letters of the alphabet:
A B C D E F G.

2. Find Middle C.

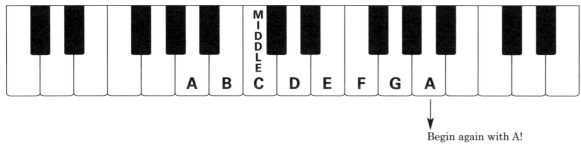

Begin again with A!

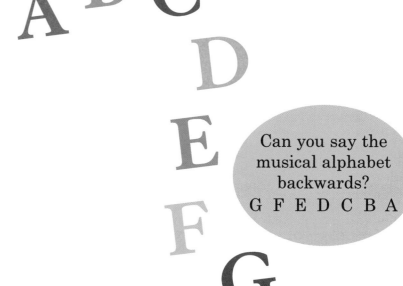

Can you say the musical alphabet backwards?
G F E D C B A

3. Using your "Perfect Piano Hand" and finger 2 of your R.H.,
play and say the letter names from Middle C **up** to the next C.
Do you hear the notes getting **higher**?

4. Using your "Perfect Piano Hand" and finger 2 of your L.H.,
play and say the letter names from Middle C **down** to the next C.
Do you hear the notes getting **lower**?

5. Say and play the seven letter names from A up with your right hand.

SAY AND PLAY THE 7 LETTER NAMES FROM A TO G EVERY DAY AT HOME. PLACE A ✔ UNDER EACH DAY YOU DO IT.

MONDAY	TUESDAY	WEDNESDAY	THURSDAY	FRIDAY	SATURDAY	SUNDAY
____	____	____	____	____	____	____

The Quarter Note ♩

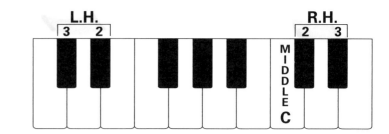

♩ This is a **quarter note**. It gets 1 beat.

Clap and step to this rhythm with a steady beat:

Each clap is 1 beat.

Before playing:

• Tap *Raindrops* on your lap, counting "1" aloud for each beat.

CD 7 • MIDI 6

Raindrops
Music by Helen Marlais
Lyrics by Helen Marlais and Kevin Olson

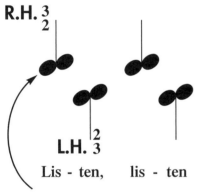

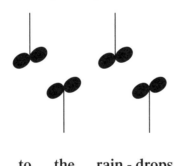

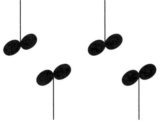

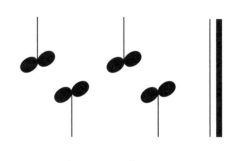

Lis - ten, lis - ten   to the rain - drops, drip - ping, drip - ping   on the roof - tops!

Play these 2 notes together!

After playing, ask yourself:

• Can I make giant raindrops? Will I play them faster or slower? Will I play them loudly or softly?

• Can I make tiny raindrops? Will I play them shorter or longer?

DUET PART: Kevin Olson (student plays 1 octave higher)

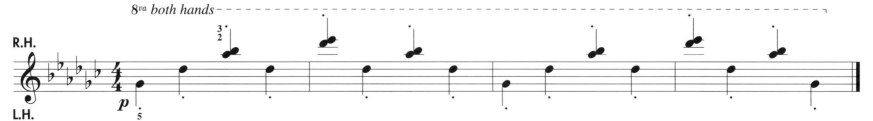

FJH2051

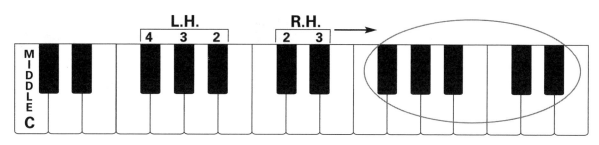

Marching

Music by Helen Marlais

Lyrics by Helen Marlais and Kevin Olson

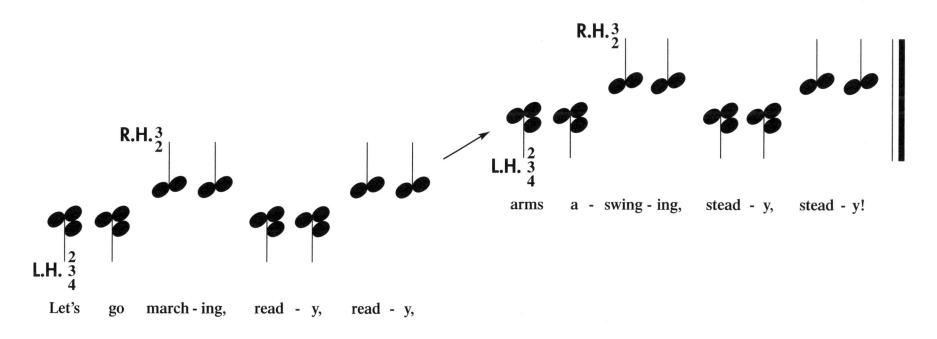

arms a - swing - ing, stead - y, stead - y!

Let's go march - ing, read - y, read - y,

DUET PART: Kevin Olson (student plays as written)

"Warm-ups for the Body" with Papa Haydn

Arm weight and flexible wrist

 REVIEW THE TECHNIQUE ON PAGES 11 AND 14.

"Drip-Drop-Roll"

- Lift your arms and let your fingers hang down, like the boy in the picture. Pretend water can **drip** through your fingertips to your thighs.

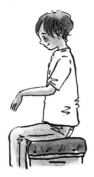

- Let your arms **drop** to your thighs. Can you feel the weight of your arms drop? (Your fingers should land flat on your legs.) This is arm weight.

- **Roll** your wrists forward onto your fingertips, and lift your wrists and forearms.

- Now drop your fingers onto any keys in front of you! (You can land flat fingered.) Did you feel your arm weight?

Just let your arms drop!

PLACE A ✓ UNDER EACH DAY YOU DO THIS "WARM-UP FOR THE BODY."						
MONDAY	TUESDAY	WEDNESDAY	THURSDAY	FRIDAY	SATURDAY	SUNDAY
ON YOUR THIGHS: ____	____	____	____	____	____	____
ON THE KEYS: ____	____	____	____	____	____	____

FJH2051

The Half Note ♩

This is a **half note**. It gets 2 beats.

1 half note = 2 quarter notes

♩ = ♩ ♩ (♥ ♥)
                       1 2

Tapping Feet
by Helen Marlais

Clap and count aloud:

1	1	1	1	1	1	1 – 2
Dance	a -	bout	with	tap -	ping	feet.

1	1	1	1	1	1	1 – 2
Step	in	time	to	feel	the	beat!

Now step and say the words!

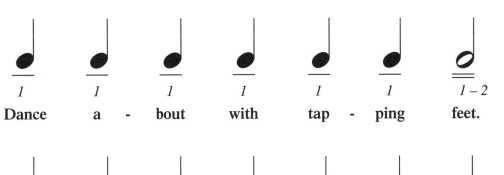

Papa Haydn says: Be sure to make the notes with 2 dashes **twice** as long as the notes with 1 dash.

Technique with Papa Haydn
Strong fingers and flexible wrist

 **REVIEW "WARM-UPS FOR THE BODY" ON PAGE 18.**

Practice this every day!

Bunnies Hop
by Helen Marlais

CD 9 • MIDI 8

1. Tap and count this rhythm:

Bun - nies   hop   ev - 'ry - where   on   our   lawn!

2. R.H.: Play fingers 2 and 3 together, going **up** the keyboard using the rhythm above.
- Drop your fingers, wrist, and forearm to the bottom of the keys as you play.
- Play the notes with a warm, big sound, saying the words as you go!
- After you play each beat, let your wrist move forward and up.

No Dent!

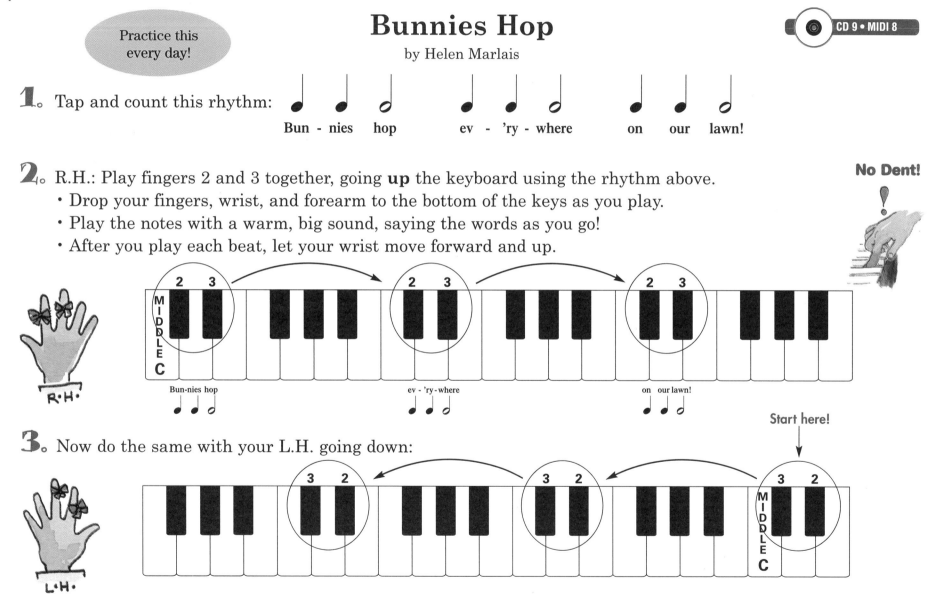

3. Now do the same with your L.H. going down:

(Students should be encouraged to memorize all the technique exercises throughout the book so they can concentrate on watching their hands and fingers while focusing on the sound they produce. The same motion of "Drip-Drop-Roll" should be used in this exercise.)

FJH2051

Music and Emotion

Music can make you feel many emotions.
What emotions are these children feeling? Circle the correct one.

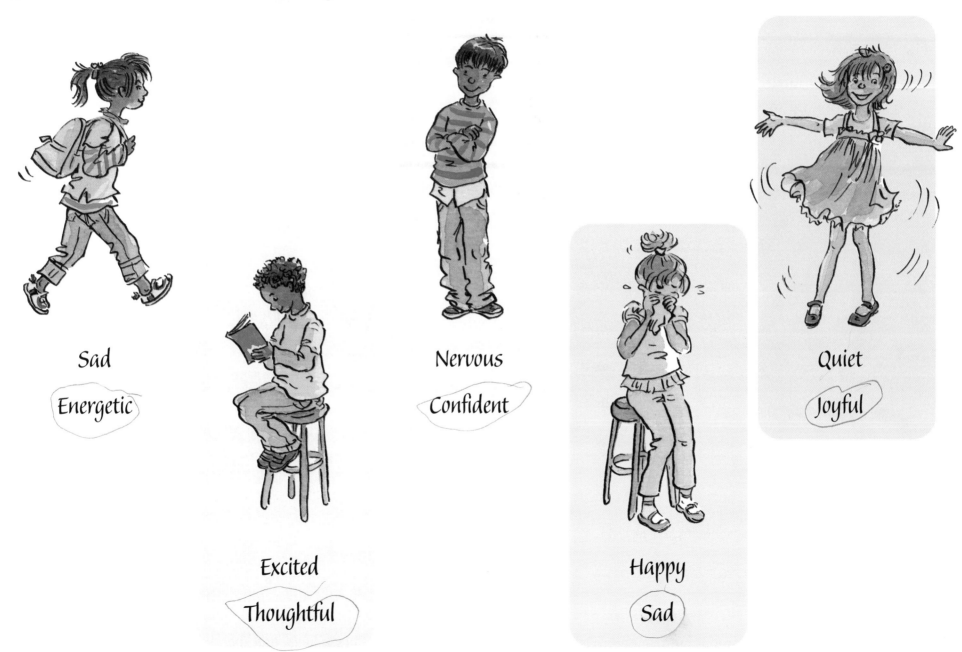

Sad

Energetic

Excited

Thoughtful

Nervous

Confident

Happy

Sad

Quiet

Joyful

Before playing:

- Circle all the ♩ (half notes).

- How many beats will a ♩ get? ___2___

  (♩ ♩ = ♩)

- Your hand will move 3 times in this piece.
  Will you move up or down? ___Up___

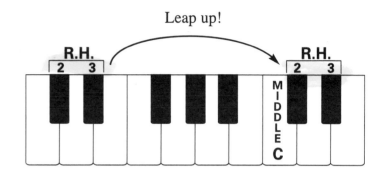

Leap up!

CD 10 • MIDI 9

Happy Frogs

Music by Helen Marlais
Lyrics by Helen Marlais and Kevin Olson

Leap up!

Leap up!

Leap up!

bugs   for   lunch!

like   to   munch,

in   their   bogs,

R.H.

Hap - py   frogs,

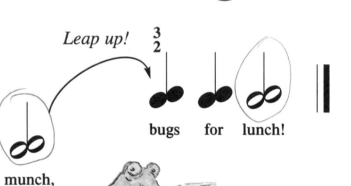

DUET PART: Kevin Olson (student plays as written)

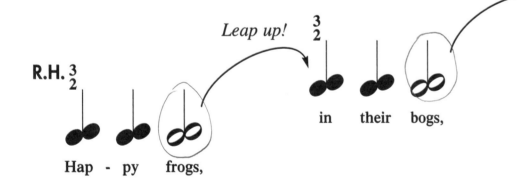

L.H.   *mp*

(Encourage students to drop their arm and wrist every time they play a group of black keys, and then lift their wrist to prepare the next group. This is the "Drip-Drop-Roll" technique.)

FJH2051

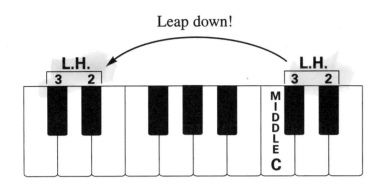

CD 11 • MIDI 10

Big Bullfrogs

by Helen Marlais

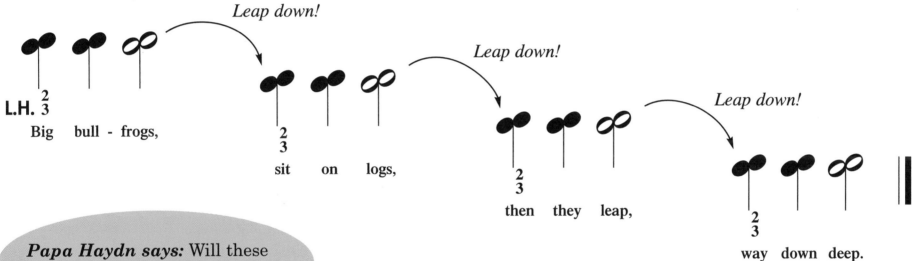

Leap down!

Leap down!

Leap down!

L.H. 2 3

Big   bull - frogs,

2 3

sit   on   logs,

2 3

then   they   leap,

2 3

way   down   deep.

Papa Haydn says: Will these pieces about frogs be loud or soft?

After playing, ask yourself:

• How are *Happy Frogs* and *Big Bullfrogs* the same? (circle one)

1) Same words 2) Same rhythm

DUET PART: Kevin Olson (student plays as written)

Melody

A **melody** is a string of notes that make a tune.
Melody is what we sing or hum!

Do you have a favorite melody?

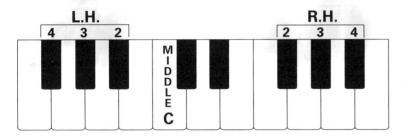

CD 12 • MIDI 11

Melodies
by Mary Leaf

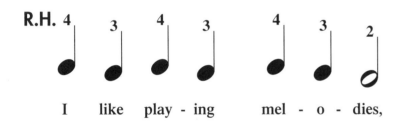

I   like   play - ing   mel - o - dies,

loud - *first time*
soft - *second time*

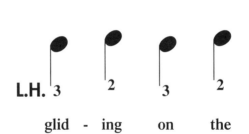

glid - ing   on   the   black   keys.

Lift your
hands off the
keys, wrists *first*,
and place them
on your lap.

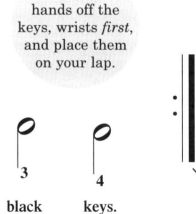

repeat sign
(Play the piece
again.)

Keep in mind!
• No dent in your fingers
• Relax your shoulders

DUET PART: Mary Leaf (student plays 1 octave higher)

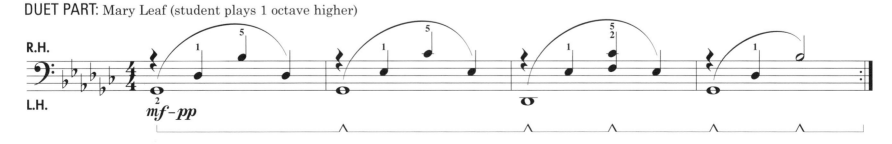

Learning CDE

Before playing:

- Play a group of 2 black keys. Then find the 3 white keys that surround it.
- Play all of the CDE's on the piano, low to high.
- On the keyboard below, circle all the groups of 2 black keys and write in all of the CDE's.

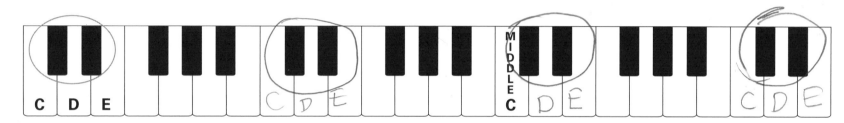

Graceful Bird

by Helen Marlais

CD 13 • MIDI 12

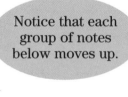

Notice that each group of notes below moves up.

R.H. 2   3   4

C   D   E

in   the   sky!

cross **L.H.** *over*

C   D   E

L.H. 4   3   2

soar - ing   high

R.H. 2   3   4

C   D   E

go - ing   by,

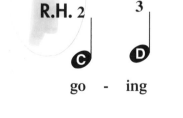

C   D   E

L.H. 4   3   2

Grace - ful   bird

After playing, ask yourself:
- Was "Graceful Bird" steady?

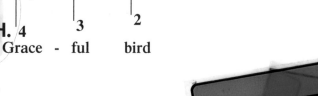

Learning Loud (*f*) and Soft (*p*)

 REVIEW THE MUSICAL ALPHABET ON PAGE 15.

forte (*f*) means to play "loudly" or "strongly." This word is Italian.

Before playing:

• Fill in the missing CDE groups on the keyboard.

Is a lion's roar loud or soft?

CD 14 • MIDI 13

A Lion!
by Helen Marlais

Go - ing on sa - fa - ri, I can see a li - on.
Just don't get too close now, or you'll soon be cry - in'!

After playing, ask yourself:
• Did I play loudly without pushing?
• Did the piece sound like a lion?

DUET PART: Kevin Olson (student plays as written)

piano (*p*) means to play "softly."
This word is Italian.

Fish in the Sea

by Helen Marlais

Are fish loud
or soft?

CD 15 • MIDI 14

R.H.

C D E D C D C
big and small, they look at me!

p

L.H.

C D E D C D E
Gen - tly swim - ming in the sea,

After playing, ask yourself:
• Did I play the melody softly while counting?
• Did the piece sound like fish in the sea?

DUET PART: Kevin Olson (student plays 1 octave higher)

R.H.

L.H. *pp*

with pedal

FJH2051

27

Repeated Notes

Recital Book p. 9

Repeated notes are a group of notes played on the same key.

Before playing:

- Circle the groups of repeated notes.
- Clap and count aloud.
- Do you think the piece should be *f* or *p*? Write *f* or *p* at the beginning of the piece, and plan the sound before you play.

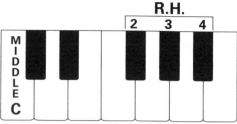

Three Black Cats

by Helen Marlais

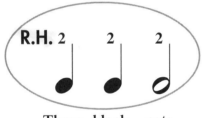 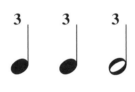  

| Three | black | cats | on | a | fence, | all | are | friends, | well | that | makes | sense! |
| Hal - low - een | | | is | so | near, | these | three | cats | will | stay | right | here! |

After playing, ask yourself:

- Did I play steadily while counting aloud?
  (Extra: Can you play *Three Black Cats* hands **together**?
  L.H. starts with finger 2.)

DUET PART: Mary Leaf (student plays 1 octave higher)

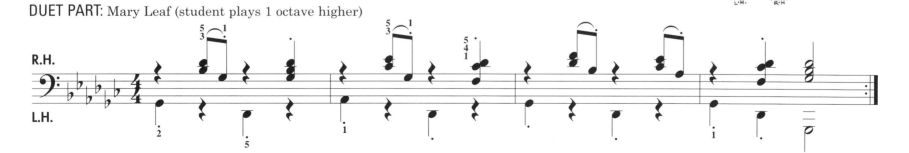

FJH2051

The Slur

The slur means to play smoothly.

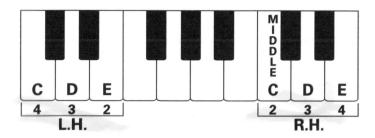

Haydn lived and worked in a palace, conducting the prince's orchestra. Here is a piece about 2 instruments— one is loud (*f*), the other soft (*p*). Playing with different **dynamics** (*f*, *p*) makes music come alive!

 Winter*

Papa Haydn's Orchestra

by Helen Marlais

 CD 17 • MIDI 16

R.H. 4 *p*
E D C D E D C
and the flute, oh what a treat!
then they'll stop and take a break!

f L.H.
E D C D E D E
2 3 4

Hear the trum - pets, tap your feet,
Lis - ten to the sounds they make,

After playing, ask yourself:
- Did I play with a steady beat?
- Did I hear *f* and *p*?

Now go back to *Fish in the Sea* and place slurs in the music. Listen to how smoothly it sounds when you play it again.

DUET PART: Helen Marlais (student plays 1 octave higher)

Technique with Papa Haydn
Two-note slurs and "Drip-Drop-Roll"

✗ **REVIEW THE TECHNIQUE ON PAGES 18 AND 20.**

Fluffy Bunny Rabbits

by Helen Marlais

CD 18 • MIDI 17

1. Tap and count the following rhythm.

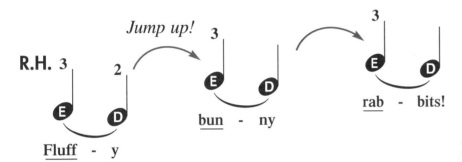

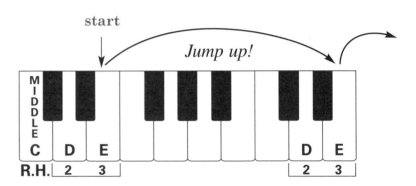

2. Drop your finger 3 on the first ♩ of each two-note slur. Let your hand, wrist, and forearm drop to the bottom of the key.

3. Play finger 2 on the second ♩, and roll your hand forward onto your fingertip. Then lift. The sound between the 2 notes should be smooth. The 1st note should be louder than the 2nd note.

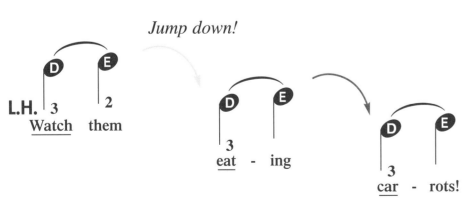

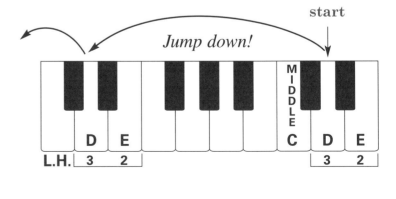

(Students should be encouraged to memorize all the technique exercises throughout the book so they can concentrate on watching their hands and fingers while focusing on the sound they produce. The motion for two-note slurs is the same as "Drip-Drop-Roll.")

FJH2051

Learning FGAB

Before playing:

- Play a group of 3 black keys. Then find the 4 white keys that surround it.
- Play all of the FGAB's on the piano, low to high, *f* to *p*.
- On the keyboard below, circle all the groups of 3 black keys and write in all of the FGAB's.

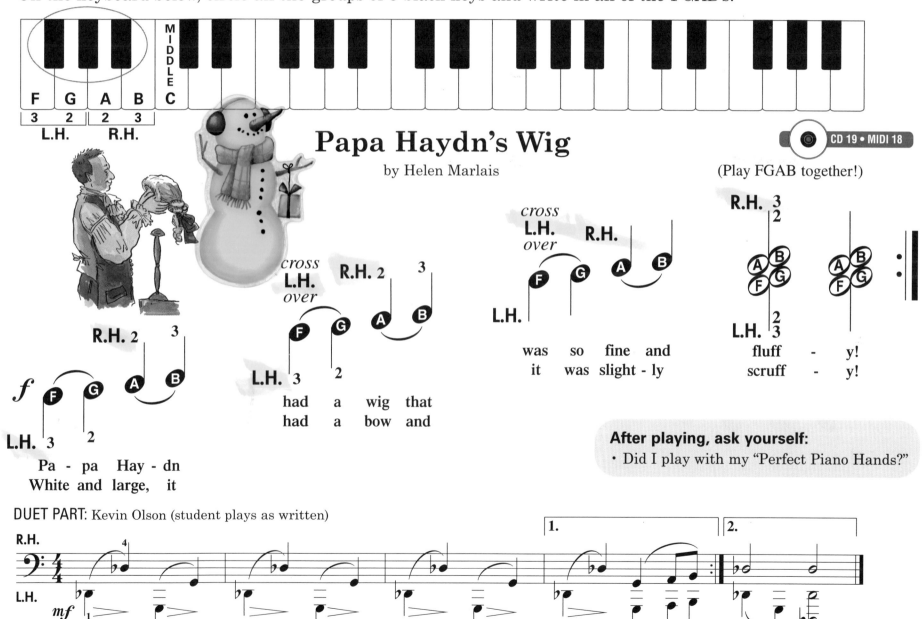

Papa Haydn's Wig

by Helen Marlais

(Play FGAB together!)

CD 19 • MIDI 18

R.H. 2 3
f **F** **G** **A** **B**
L.H. 3 2
Pa - pa Hay - dn
White and large, it

cross
L.H.
over
F **G**
R.H. 2 3
A **B**
L.H. 3 2
had a wig that
had a bow and

cross
L.H.
over
F **G**
R.H.
A **B**
L.H.
was so fine and
it was slight - ly

R.H. 3 2
A **B**
F **G**
A **B**
F **G**
L.H. 2 3
fluff - y!
scruff - y!

After playing, ask yourself:
- Did I play with my "Perfect Piano Hands?"

DUET PART: Kevin Olson (student plays as written)

R.H.

L.H. *mf*

Bar Lines

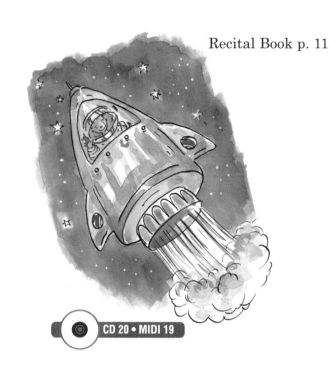

Bar lines look like this: | | Do you see them in this piece? The space between the bar lines is called a MEASURE. Placing bar lines in the music helps to group the beats so the same number of beats are in each measure. | measure | measure |

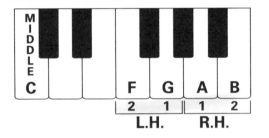

White Christmas
Yellow Spaceship
by Kevin Olson

CD 20 • MIDI 19

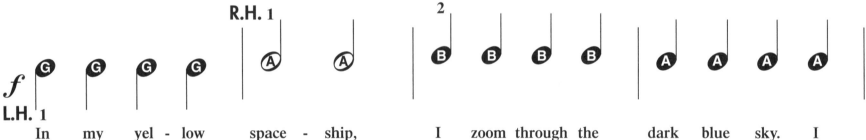

f

L.H. 1

R.H. 1

2

G G G G | A A | B B B B | A A A A |

In my yel - low space - ship, I zoom through the dark blue sky. I

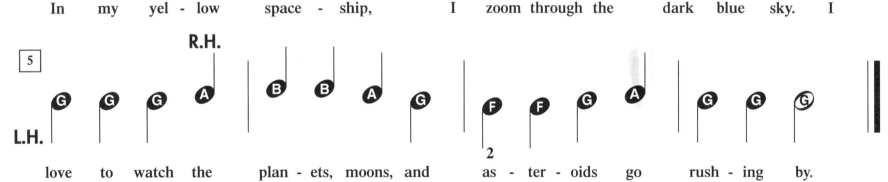

5

L.H.

R.H.

G G G A | B B A G | F F G A | G G G |

love to watch the plan - ets, moons, and as - ter - oids go rush - ing by.

DUET PART: Kevin Olson (student plays 1 octave higher)

R.H.

L.H. *mf*

ped. simile

FJH2051

Before playing:

- Listen to your teacher play this piece.
- Make a rainbow in the air to show the phrasing, like this:
- Starting with your R.H. in front of your left shoulder, slowly make a rainbow in the air from left to right to show the shape of the phrase.

A slur ⌢ shows you a musical idea, called a **phrase**. Play phrases smoothly.

Butterflies

by Helen Marlais

CD 21 • MIDI 20

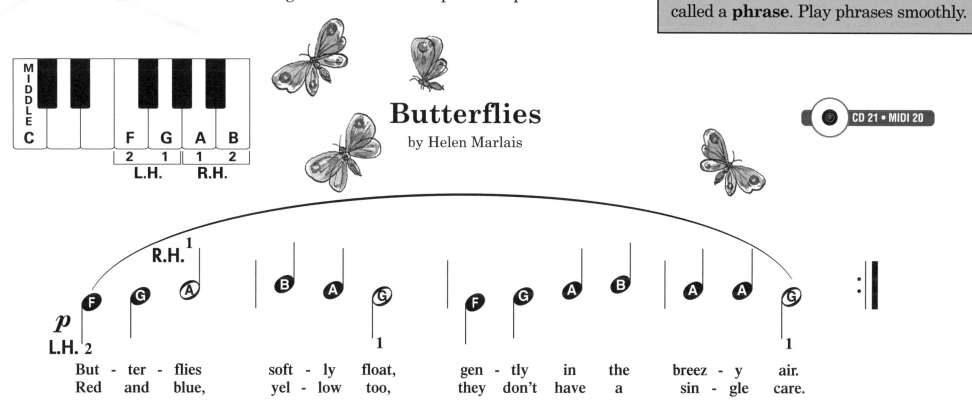

But - ter - flies   soft - ly   float,   gen - tly   in   the   breez - y   air.
Red   and   blue,   yel - low   too,   they   don't   have   a   sin - gle   care.

After playing, ask yourself:
- Did I play smoothly and softly?

DUET PART: Timothy Brown (student plays as written)

The Whole Note o

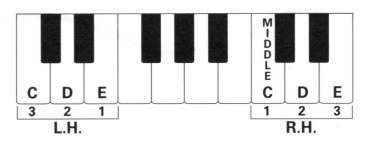

o This is a **whole note**. It gets 4 beats.

o = ♩ ♩ ♩ ♩ (♥ ♥ ♥ ♥)
     1 2 3 4

Before playing:

• Circle the **o** in this piece.

"Feel the same motion!"

Mary Had a Little Lamb

Traditional
Arranged by Helen Marlais

 CD 22 • MIDI 21

R.H. 3

f

Mar - y   had   a   lit - tle   lamb,   lit - tle   lamb,   lit - tle   lamb,
Ev - 'ry - where that   Mar - y   went,   Mar - y   went,   Mar - y   went,

DUET PART: Timothy Brown (student plays 1 octave higher)

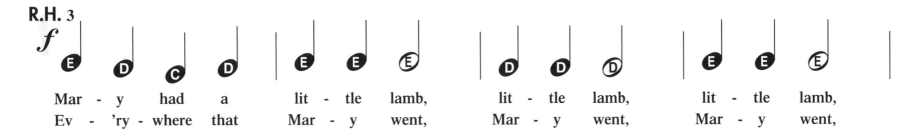

         FJH2051

It's Matching Time!

Draw a line from the left to the correct answer on the right.

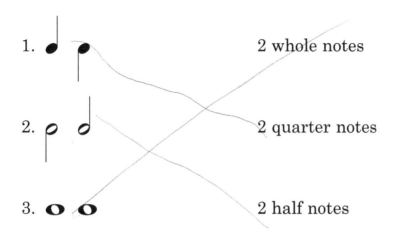

1. 2 whole notes

2. 2 quarter notes

3. 2 half notes

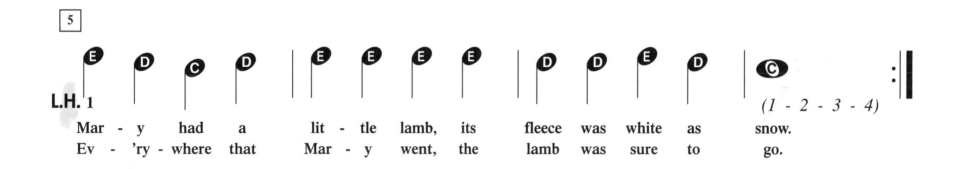

5

L.H. 1

E D C D | E E E E | D D E D | C :||

(1 - 2 - 3 - 4)

Mar - y had a lit - tle lamb, its fleece was white as snow.
Ev - 'ry - where that Mar - y went, the lamb was sure to go.

(Encourage students to review "Perfect Piano Hands" on pages 5 and 14, as well as "Drip-Drop-Roll" on page 18.)

Learning CDEF

Before playing:

- Tap and count the rhythm aloud.
- How many phrases are there? _____
- Form your "Perfect Piano Hands."

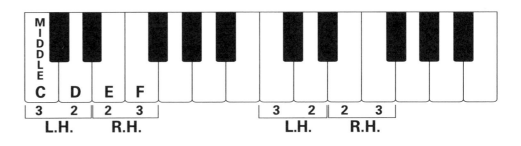

CD 23 • MIDI 22

Move both hands up to the next C D E F.

Blowing Bubbles

by Helen Marlais

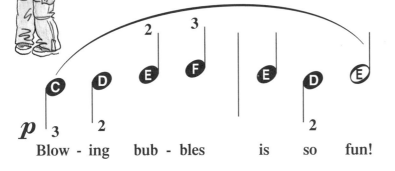 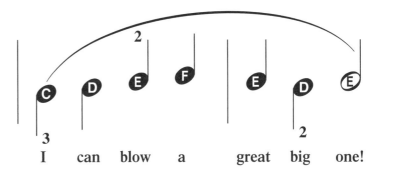

Blow - ing bub - bles is so fun!   I can blow a   great big one!

DUET PART: Timothy Brown (student plays 1 octave higher)

FJH2051

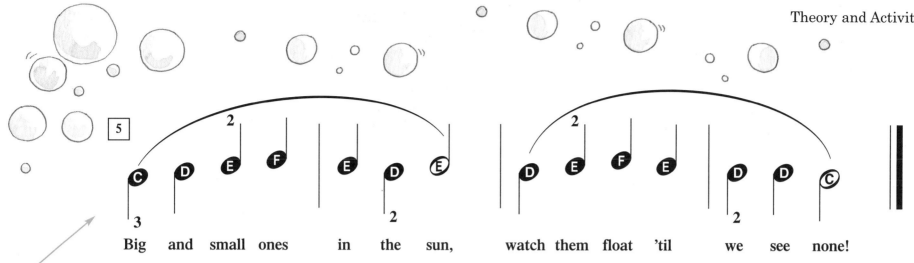

Big and small ones in the sun, watch them float 'til we see none!

Discovering 2nds (steps)

1.

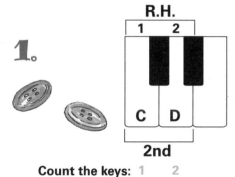

Place a button on a C on the keyboard. Then place a button on the next key higher, D.

The distance from 1 white key to the next white key is a 2nd.

Starting on C with finger number 1, count up to D. It's a 2nd!

2.

Soon you will learn all about notes on lines and spaces.

This is a note on a line: ━○━ This note is on a space: ▭○▭

This is a 2nd: ○○ (line to space).

This is also a 2nd: ○○ (space to line). 2nds are also called steps.

Papa Haydn says:
Notice the 2nds in
Blowing Bubbles.

Technique with Papa Haydn

The Time Signature

> The **time signature** at the beginning of the piece tells you the number of beats in each measure.
>
> **4** The upper 4 means there are 4 beats in every measure.
> **4** The bottom 4 means a ♩ receives one beat.

"Feel the same motion!"

Before playing:

- Circle the time signature below.
- Step to the beat and count aloud.
- Are the steps going up or down?
- Tap and count aloud.

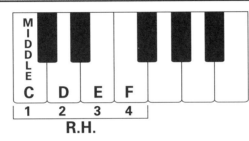

No Dent!

CD 24 • MIDI 23

Keep in Mind! Strong Fingers
by Helen Marlais

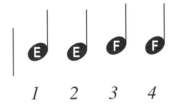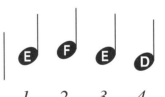

R.H. 1
4/4

C	C	C	C	D	D	D		E	E	F	F	E	F	E	D		C		:		
1	2	3	4	1	2	3	4	1	2	3	4	1	2	3	4	1	2	3	4
I	am	play-ing		with-out	dents,			and	I	watch	my	"Per-fect	Pia-no			Hand!"

L·H·

- Now play *Keep in Mind! Strong Fingers* with your L.H.
- Start with finger 4.

Now try it hands together!

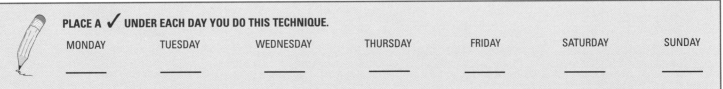

PLACE A ✓ UNDER EACH DAY YOU DO THIS TECHNIQUE.

MONDAY	TUESDAY	WEDNESDAY	THURSDAY	FRIDAY	SATURDAY	SUNDAY
___	___	___	___	___	___	___

FJH2051

Before playing:

- Add the bar lines after every 4 beats.
- Circle all the repeated notes. Notice that this piece is made up of 2nds and repeated notes.
- Tap the rhythm and speak the words with energy!

Autumn Leaves

by Helen Marlais

CD 25 • MIDI 24

Lift your hands off the keys, wrists *first*, and place them on your lap.

DUET PART: Mary Leaf (student plays 1 octave higher)

(Can your students play this piece in 3 different locations on the piano—high, middle, and low?)

Learning C Position

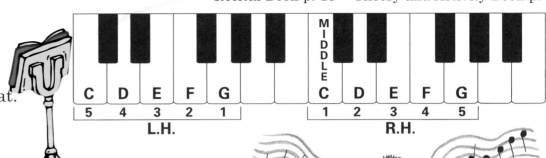

Before playing:

- Clap and count the rhythm aloud with a steady beat.
- Point to the notes and count aloud.
  Then point and say the words.
- Plan your "Perfect Piano Hands" and the f sound.

All Five Fingers, C to G!

by Helen Marlais

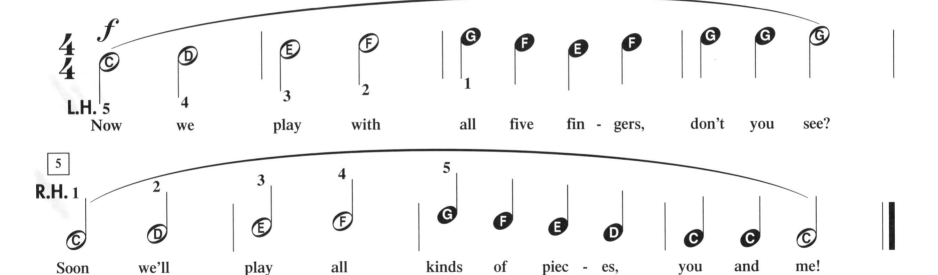

L.H.
Now   we   play   with   all   five   fin - gers,   don't   you   see?

R.H.
Soon   we'll   play   all   kinds   of   piec - es,   you   and   me!

After playing, ask yourself:
- Did I play with a f sound?
- Did I count steadily?

DUET PART: Kevin Olson (student plays 1 octave higher)

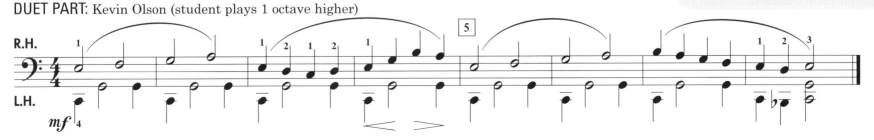

FJH2051

Discovering 3rds

1.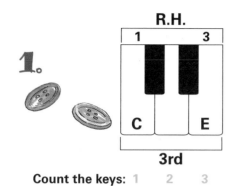

Place a button on Middle C.

Going higher, **skip 1 key** and place a button on the E.

The distance between a white key to another white key, with 1 white key **skipped** in the middle, is a 3rd.

Starting on C with finger number 1, count up to E. It's a 3rd!

2.

Draw an X on the key a 3rd below A. Then play this 3rd on the piano.

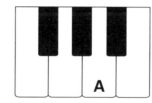

3. You have learned that  and are 2nds.

This is a 3rd:

This is also a 3rd:

Draw a 3rd above the line note:

Draw a 3rd above the space note:

Before playing:

Recital Book p. 16 • Theory and Activity Book p. 30, 31

- Circle all the 3rds. The 1st one has been done for you.
- Find and play them on the piano.
- Plan the dynamics.

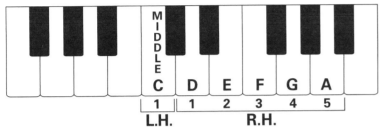

Bluebird

Traditional
Arranged by Helen Marlais

CD 27 • MIDI 26

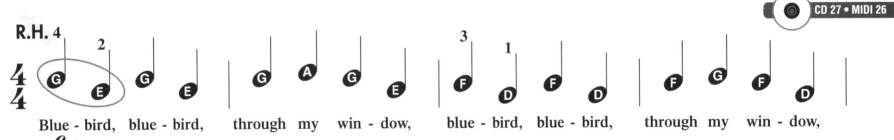

Blue - bird, blue - bird, through my win - dow, blue - bird, blue - bird, through my win - dow,

f first time
p second time

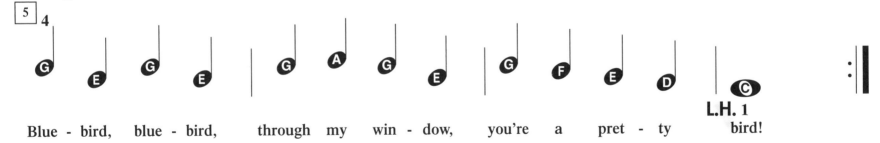

Blue - bird, blue - bird, through my win - dow, you're a pret - ty bird!

L.H. 1

DUET PART: Timothy Brown (student plays 1 octave higher)

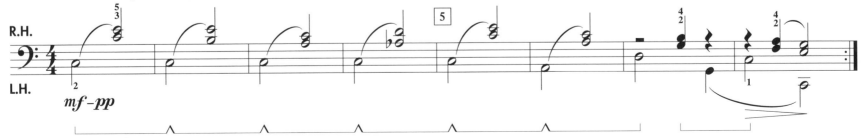

mf–pp

FJH2051

Discovering 4ths

Place a button on G on the keyboard.

Going higher, **skip 2 keys** and place a button on C.

Starting on G with finger number 1, count up to the C. It's a 4th!

On lines and spaces, a 4th looks like this: 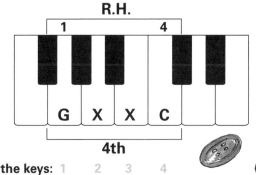 or this:

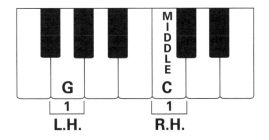

Count the keys: 1 2 3 4

Giants
by Helen Marlais

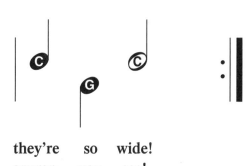

CD 28 • MIDI 27

R.H. 1

4/4 *f*

L.H. 1

| Gi | - | ants | | just | can't | hide! | | That's | 'cause | | they're | so | wide! |
| Big | - | ger | | than | a | tree, | | he's | a | | grump, | you | see! |

After playing, ask yourself:
• Did I play *forte?*

DUET PART: Timothy Brown (student plays 1 octave higher)

R.H.

5

9: 4/4

L.H. *mf* 3

8va - - - - - - - - - - - - - - - - - - -

The Dotted Half Note 𝅗𝅥.

𝅗𝅥. This is a **dotted half note**. It gets 3 beats. 𝅗𝅥. = ♩ ♩ ♩ (♥ ♥ ♥)
　　　　　　　　　　　　　　　　　　　　　　　　　　 1　2　3

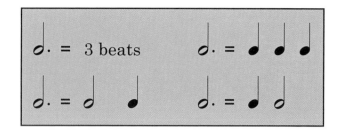

Before playing:

- Make a rainbow in the air to show the 2 phrases as your teacher plays *Stars in the Sky*.

- Do you hear 3 beats or 4 beats in every measure? _____

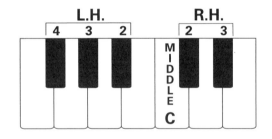

Stars in the Sky

by Helen Marlais

3 = 3 beats in every measure
4 = ♩ gets 1 beat

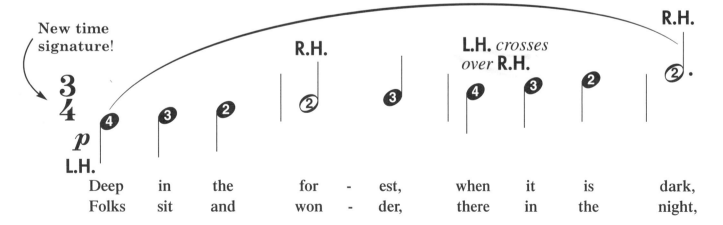

New time signature!

3
4

p

L.H.

R.H.

L.H. *crosses over* R.H.

R.H.

| Deep | in | the | for | - | est, | when | it | is | dark, |
| Folks | sit | and | won | - | der, | there | in | the | night, |

44　　　　　　　　　　　　　　　　　　　　　　　　　　　　　　　　　FJH2051

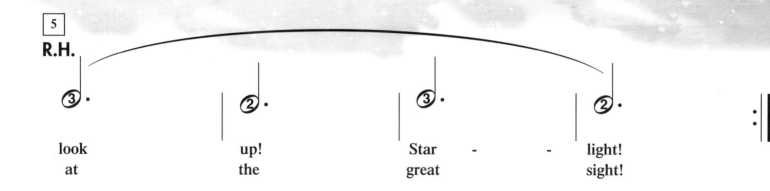

5

R.H.

look   up!   Star   -   -   light!
at   the   great   sight!

After learning this piece:
- Can you play *Stars in the Sky* starting higher on the piano and even more quietly?
- If you can reach the pedal on the right with your right foot, press it down throughout the entire piece and listen to the sound!

DUET PART: Timothy Brown (student plays 1 octave higher)

Technique with Papa Haydn
Arm weight and flexible wrist

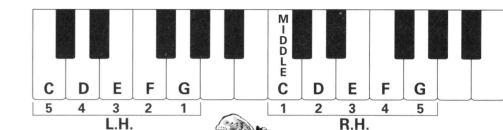

 REVIEW THE TECHNIQUE ON PAGES 30 AND 38.

"Feel the same motion!"

♥ **Wrist Dance**

by Helen Marlais

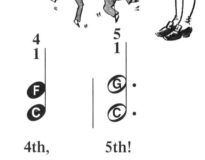

Imagine Papa Haydn pulling a string up gently from your wrist after you play each beat.

CD 30 • MIDI 29

Slowly

R.H. *Start with finger 1 on Middle C.*

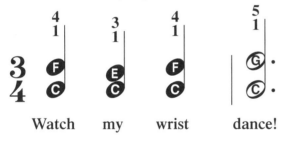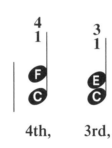

Watch   my   wrist   dance!   4th,   3rd,   4th,   5th!

Slowly

L.H. *Start with C and F below Middle C.*

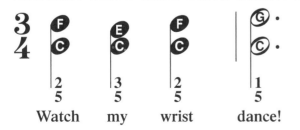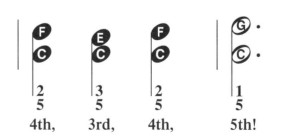

Watch   my   wrist   dance!   4th,   3rd,   4th,   5th!

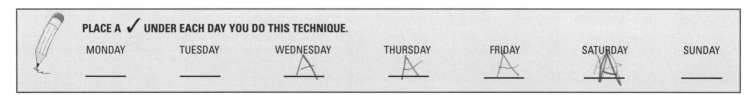

PLACE A ✔ UNDER EACH DAY YOU DO THIS TECHNIQUE.

MONDAY	TUESDAY	WEDNESDAY	THURSDAY	FRIDAY	SATURDAY	SUNDAY
		A	A	A	A	

FJH2051

The Staff

1. This is a STAFF. It has 5 lines and 4 spaces.

2. This is a GRAND STAFF.

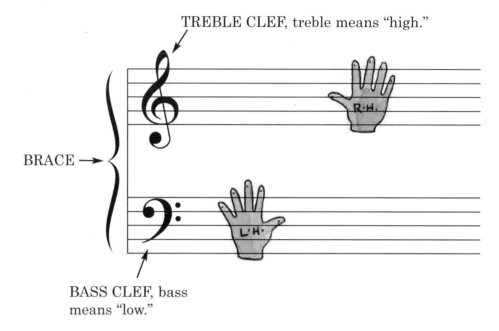

TREBLE CLEF, treble means "high."

BRACE →

BASS CLEF, bass means "low."

3. Middle C is always in the middle of the Grand Staff, written on a short line. These lines are called LEDGER LINES.

4. Middle C is a very important note. It's called a **Guide Note.**
- Below, draw 4 space notes in the Treble staff.
- Then, draw 5 line notes in the Bass staff.

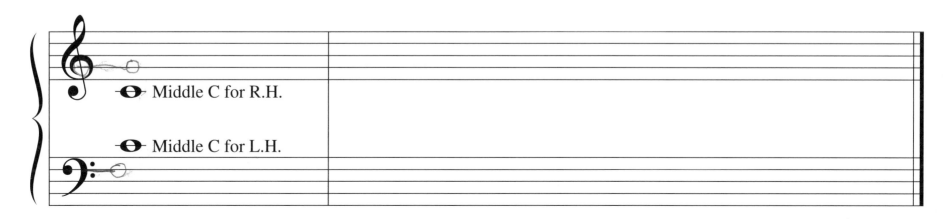

Middle C for R.H.

Middle C for L.H.

Before playing:

- Step to and count the rhythm aloud.
- Tap the rhythm and speak the words with energy!

CD 31 • MIDI 30

Middle C Position

The Middle C High Step

by Helen Marlais

Happily

f Mid - dle C is here; Let's step in - to gear.

Hoo - ray! Hoo - ray! C's are fun to play!

Lift your hands off the keys, wrists first, and place them on your lap.

DUET PART: Mary Leaf (student plays as written)

R.H.

L.H. *mf*

FJH2051

Technique on the Grand Staff with Papa Haydn
Learning 3 Guide Notes

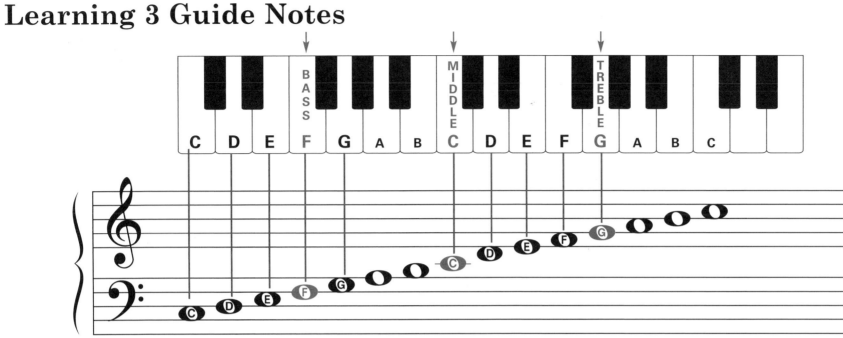

Guide Notes

CD 32 • MIDI 31

by Helen Marlais

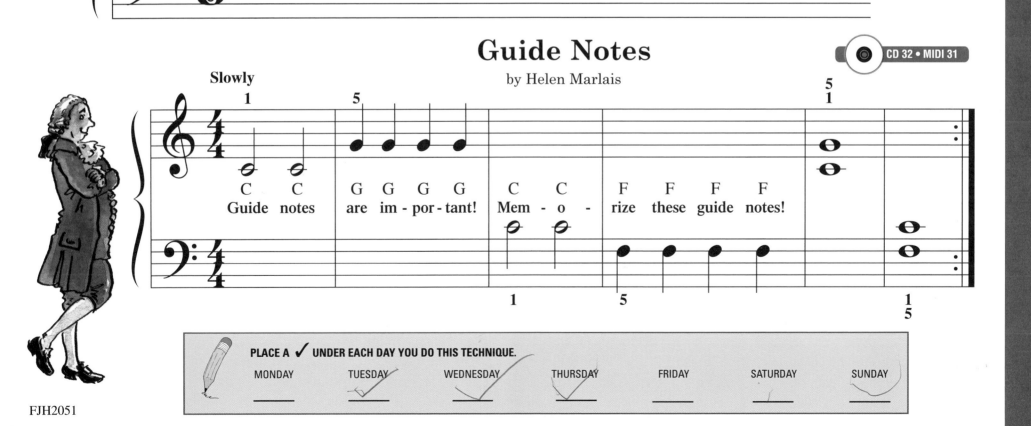

Slowly

C C
Guide notes

G G G G
are im - por - tant!

C C
Mem - o -

F F F F
rize these guide notes!

PLACE A ✔ UNDER EACH DAY YOU DO THIS TECHNIQUE.

MONDAY	TUESDAY	WEDNESDAY	THURSDAY	FRIDAY	SATURDAY	SUNDAY
____	____	____	____	____	____	____

Middle C and Treble G

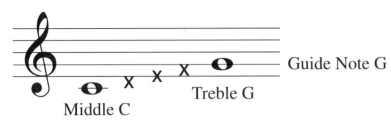

Middle C

Treble G

Guide Note G

The **Treble Clef** has another name—**G Clef**, because it shows a special G on the staff.

Discovering 5ths

From Middle C **up** to Treble G is a 5th. Place a button on C, and another one on G. Notice that you **skip 3 keys**. Do you see that you skip 3 notes on the staff?

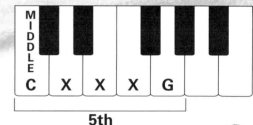

Count the keys: 1 2 3 4 5

CD 33 • MIDI 32

A Rainbow

by Kevin Olson

Brightly

Look - ing out my win - dow, I can see a rain - bow,

Arch - ing oh so grace - ful - ly a - cross the sky.

After playing, ask yourself:
- Did I hear what I expected to hear?
- Did I play with my "Perfect Piano Hands?"

DUET PART: Kevin Olson (student plays 1 octave higher)

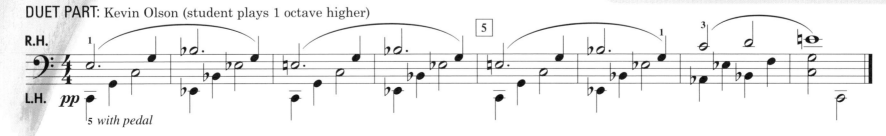

with pedal

FJH2051

Middle C and Bass F

Discovering 5ths

From Middle C **down** to Bass F is a 5th. Place a button on C, and another one on F. Notice that you **skip 3 keys**. Do you see that you skip 3 notes on the staff?

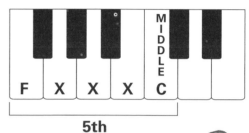

The **Bass Clef** has another name—**F Clef**, because it shows a special F on the staff.

 **CD 34 • MIDI 33**

Moonlight
by Kevin Olson

Count the keys: 1 2 3 4 5

Peacefully

L.H. 1   5

p Look - ing   out   my   win - dow,   I   can   see   the   moon   glow,

Gen - tly   giv - ing   light   to   all   the   world   be - low.

DUET PART: Kevin Olson (student plays 1 octave higher)

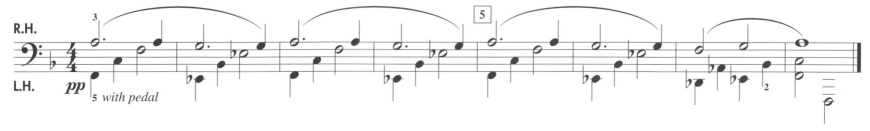

R.H.

L.H.   *pp*   5 *with pedal*

Before playing:

- Block (play together) Guide Notes Middle C and Treble G with your R.H.

- Then, block Guide Notes Middle C and Bass F with your L.H.

City Sounds

by Kevin Costley

CD 35 • MIDI 34

Middle C Position

Hear those loud | cit - y sounds; | BEEP! BEEP! | all a - round.

Fire trucks and | si - ren sounds; | SO LOUD | o - ver town.

DUET PART: Kevin Costley (student plays 1 octave higher)

(Encourage students to review the techniques on pages 5, 18, and 49 in order to form "Perfect Piano Hands" and use arm weight when playing 5ths.)

Before playing:

- How many phrases are in this piece? _____
- Clap and count aloud with energy.
- Tap and say the words.

The Big Parade

by Kevin Costley

CD 36 • MIDI 35

Middle C Position

With energy

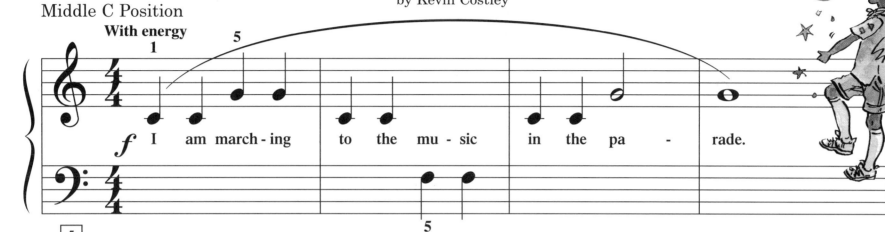

f   I   am march-ing   to   the   mu - sic   in   the   pa   -   rade.

All   my   friends   see   me   now.   What   a   blast!   Hur   -   ray!

After playing, ask yourself:
- Did I count steadily?
- Was the piece *forte*?

DUET PART: Kevin Costley (student plays 1 octave higher)

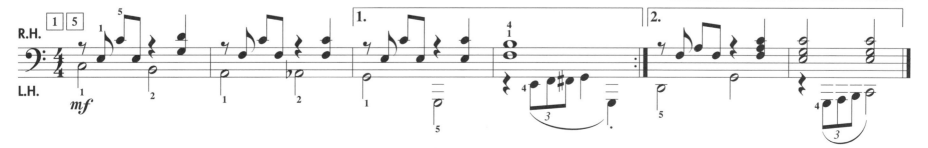

UNIT 9

Learning GAB in the L.H.

Before playing:

- Notice Bass G is a 2nd up from Guide Note F.
- Find each 2nd in the piece below. Say aloud if it goes up or goes down.
- Say the letter name of each note.

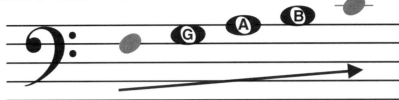

2nds going up

CD 37 • MIDI 36

I Like Eating Spinach

by Helen Marlais

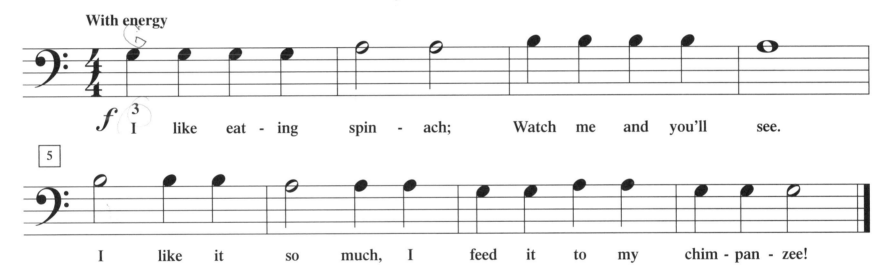

With energy

f

I   like   eat - ing   spin - ach;   Watch   me   and   you'll   see.

I   like   it   so   much,   I   feed   it   to   my   chim - pan - zee!

After playing, ask yourself:

- Did I hold the 𝅗𝅥 for 2 beats?
- Did I play with a steady beat?

DUET PART: Edwin McLean (student plays as written)

R.H. *mf*

L.H. *mp*

FJH2051

Learning DEF in the R.H.

Before playing:

- Notice that D is a 2nd up from Guide Note Middle C.
- Find each 2nd in the piece below.
  Say aloud if it goes up or goes down.
- Point to the notes and count aloud.
  Then point and speak the words in rhythm.
- Say the letter name of each note.

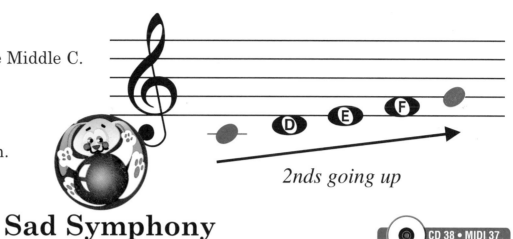

2nds going up

Sad Symphony

by Kevin Olson and Helen Marlais

CD 38 · MIDI 37

Slowly

p Sad, sad sym - pho - ny, it has a mel - o - dy that

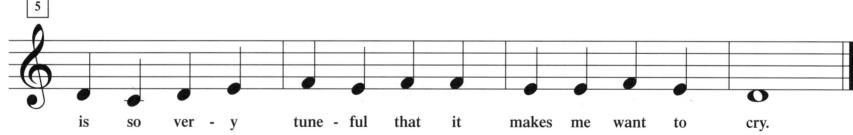

is so ver - y tune - ful that it makes me want to cry.

After playing, ask yourself:

- Did I hold the 𝅗𝅥. for 3 beats?
- Did I hear what I expected to hear?

DUET PART: Kevin Olson (student plays as written)

Before playing:

- Point to each note and count aloud. Then point and say the words.
- Circle the Guide Note Middle C's.
- Find and play the B's in the Bass Clef.

"Clickity Clack" Went the Carriage

Music by Kevin Olson
Lyrics by Helen Marlais

Imagine what it would be like to have to travel long distances riding in a carriage with horses! Papa Haydn had to!

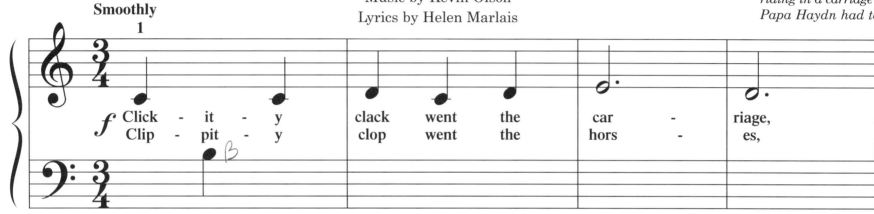

Smoothly

Click - it - y clack went the car - riage,
Clip - pit - y clop went the the hors - es,

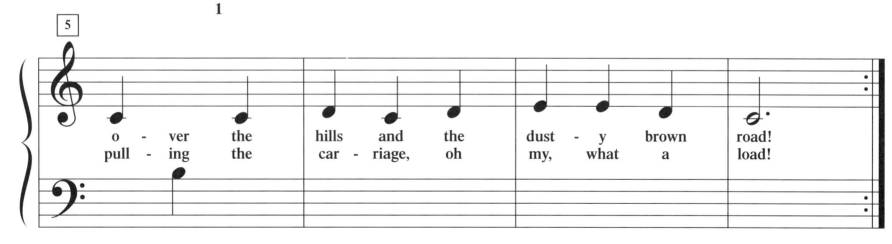

o - ver the hills and the dust - y brown road!
pull - ing the car - riage, oh my, what a load!

DUET PART: Kevin Olson (student plays 1 octave higher)

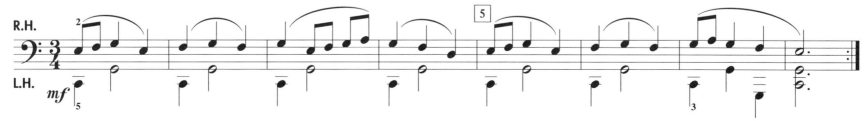

R.H.

L.H.

FJH2051

Before playing:

- Say the letter name of each note.
- Find the 2nds.
- Tap the rhythm while you say the words.
- Circle the dynamics (*f*, *p*).

Sharing C
by Helen Marlais

Be sure to drop your arm weight on all the Middle C's for a big, warm sound.

 CD 40 • MIDI 39

Middle C Position

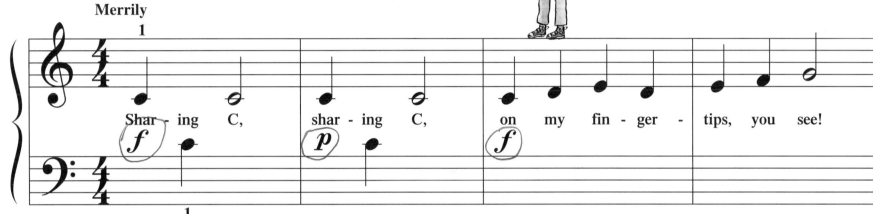

Merrily

Shar - ing C, shar - ing C, on my fin - ger - tips, you see!

f   *p*   *f*

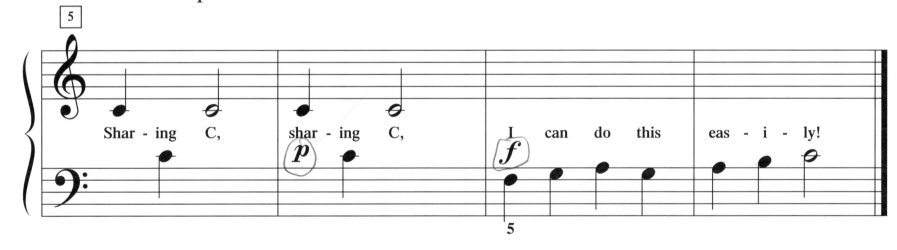

Shar - ing C, shar - ing C, I can do this eas - i - ly!

p   *f*

DUET PART: Timothy Brown (student plays 1 octave higher)

R.H.

L.H.   *mf*   *pp*   *mf*   *pp*   *mf*

Before playing:

- Should *Big Black Bear* be f or p? Mark it in the begin iece.
- Find and play the B's, A's, and G's in the Bass Clef.

Big Black Bear

Music by Timothy Brown
Lyrics by Helen Marlais

CD 41 • MIDI 40

Middle C Position

Heavily

Nev - er   feed   a   big,   black   bear,

'cause   he'll   come   back,   what   a   scare!

DUET PART: Timothy Brown (student plays as written)

R.H.

L.H.

FJH2051

9

He's   so   smart,   he'll   al - ways   know,

13

where   the   food   is,   high   or   low!

Lift your hands off the keys, wrists *first*, and place them on your lap.

After playing, ask yourself:
- Did the piece sound like the title? Why?
- Where are the 2nds? Where is the *only* 5th?

Technique with Papa Haydn

Playing 3rds and weight transfer

CD 42 • MIDI 41

Stand up and shift your weight from one leg to the other. This is weight transfer. When you play, transfer the weight of your arm from 1 finger to the next.

• Circle the fingers you will use in your L.H.

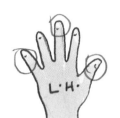

Start on F, then to A, up to C, back to F!

• Circle the fingers you will use in your R.H.

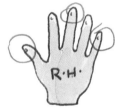

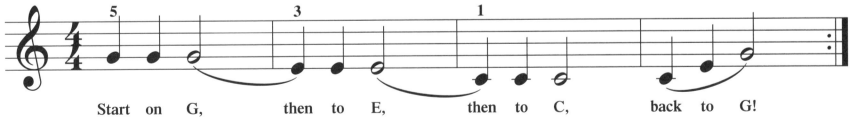

Start on G, then to E, then to C, back to G!

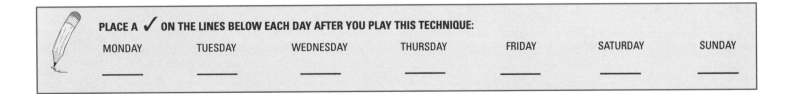

PLACE A ✓ ON THE LINES BELOW EACH DAY AFTER YOU PLAY THIS TECHNIQUE:

MONDAY	TUESDAY	WEDNESDAY	THURSDAY	FRIDAY	SATURDAY	SUNDAY
_____	_____	_____	_____	_____	_____	_____

FJH2051

Before playing:

- Circle the 3rds in *Piano Polka*:
- Tap and count the rhythm and then say the words aloud!

Middle C Position

Piano Polka

by Kevin Olson

CD 43 • MIDI 42

Happily

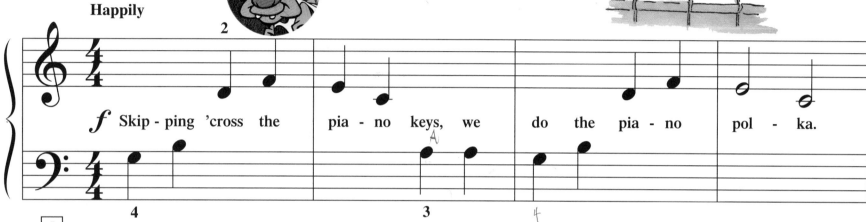

f Skip - ping 'cross the | pia - no keys, we | do the pia - no | pol - ka.

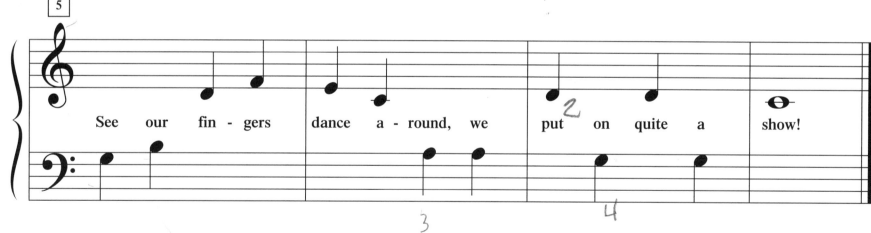

See our fin - gers | dance a - round, we | put on quite a | show!

DUET PART: Kevin Olson (student plays 1 octave higher)

R.H.

L.H. *mf*

Before playing:

- Prepare your fingers over the keys.
- Find the 2nds in the music.
  Play the 2nds blocked (together.)
- Now find the 3rds.
  One has been circled for you.
  Play the 3rds blocked (together).

Stephen Foster was an American composer who was born in Pittsburgh, Pennsylvania in 1827. He was self-taught and wrote over 200 songs!

Camptown Races

by Stephen Foster
Arranged by Helen Marlais

CD 44 • MIDI 43

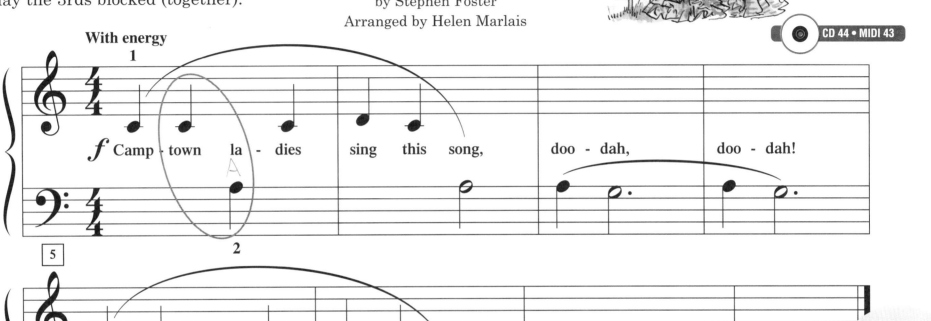

With energy

Camp - town la - dies sing this song, doo - dah, doo - dah!

Camp - town race track five miles long, oh, doo - dah day!

Lift your hands off the keys, wrists *first*, and place them on your lap.

DUET PART: Timothy Brown (student plays 1 octave higher)

R.H.

L.H.

FJH2051

Before playing:

- There is one 5th in the L.H. Circle it and then block it (play the notes at the same time).
- There are two 5ths in the R.H. Circle them and then block them.
- Notice that you are in C Position.

Waterfalls

Music by Ferdinand Beyer
(adapted)
1803-1863, Germany
Lyrics by Helen Marlais

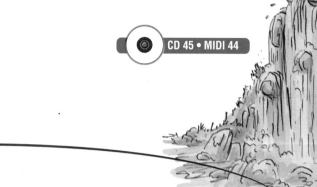

CD 45 • MIDI 44

C Position

Merrily

In the sum-mer - time, we go to plac - es with big wa - ter - falls, and

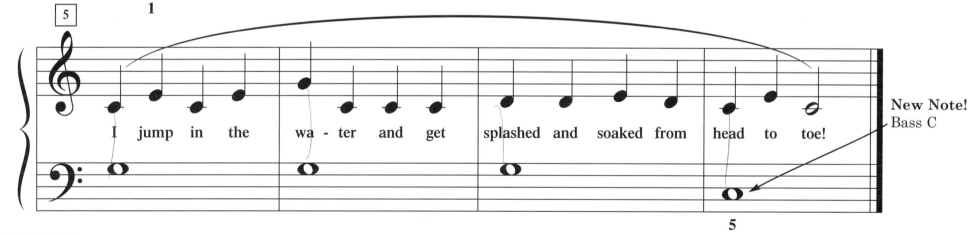

I jump in the wa - ter and get splashed and soaked from head to toe!

New Note!
Bass C

DUET PART: Timothy Brown (student plays 2 octaves higher)

Playing 4ths

Before playing:

· Can you find the 4ths in *The Bagpipes*?

· Look at the 4 phrases.
How are they the same?
How are they different?

A 4th has 2 **skipped** notes. It looks like this:

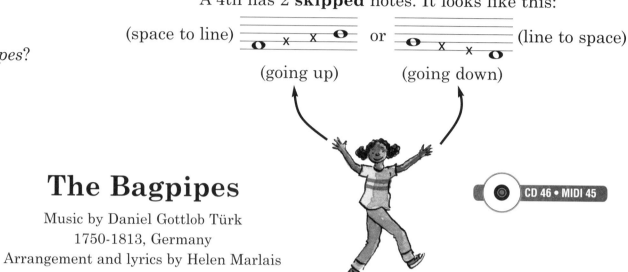

(space to line) or (line to space)

(going up) (going down)

The Bagpipes

Music by Daniel Gottlob Türk
1750-1813, Germany
Arrangement and lyrics by Helen Marlais

CD 46 · MIDI 45

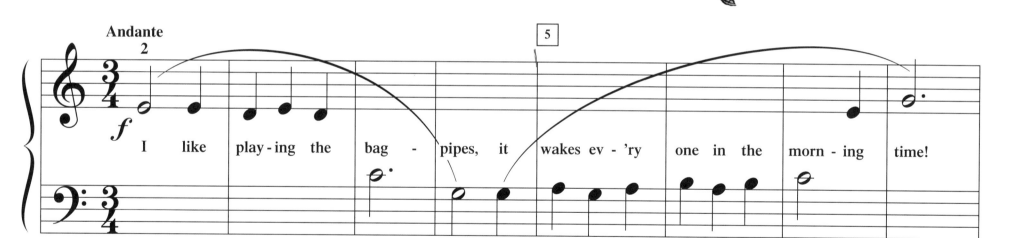

Andante

I like play-ing the bag - pipes, it wakes ev - 'ry one in the morn - ing time!

DUET PART: Timothy Brown (student plays 1 octave higher)

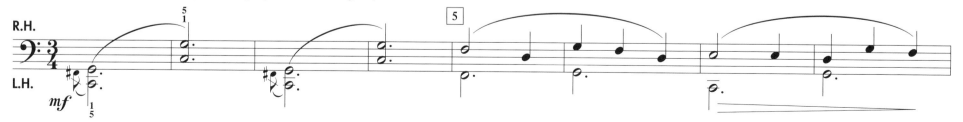

R.H.

L.H.

FJH2051

This is a small bagpipes. Different kinds of bagpipes have been played for over 400 years!

Tempo marking:
Andante is an Italian word that means "walking" speed. Feel calm and comfortable when playing at an *andante* speed.

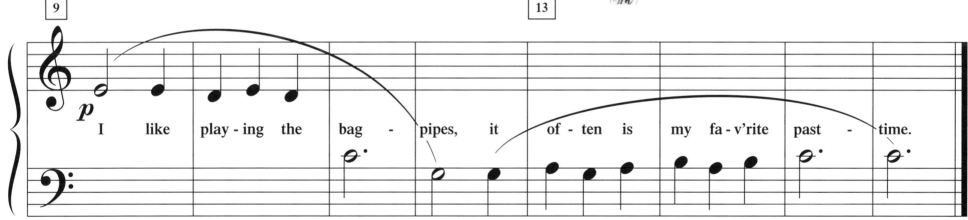

I like play - ing the bag - pipes, it of - ten is my fa - v'rite past - time.

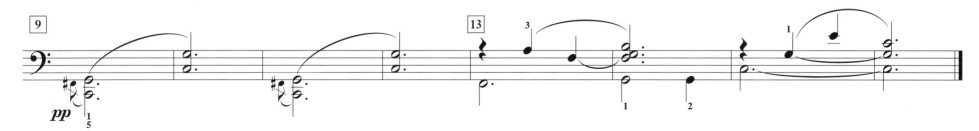

65

Technique with Papa Haydn

Arm and wrist rotation

 REVIEW THE TECHNIQUE ON PAGE 60 AND ANY OTHER PAGES YOUR TEACHER ASSIGNS: _____.

Play the next 2 warm-ups with strong fingers. Rock your arm and wrist from side to side slowly, like a boat rocking gently from side to side.

Rocking the Boat

by Helen Marlais

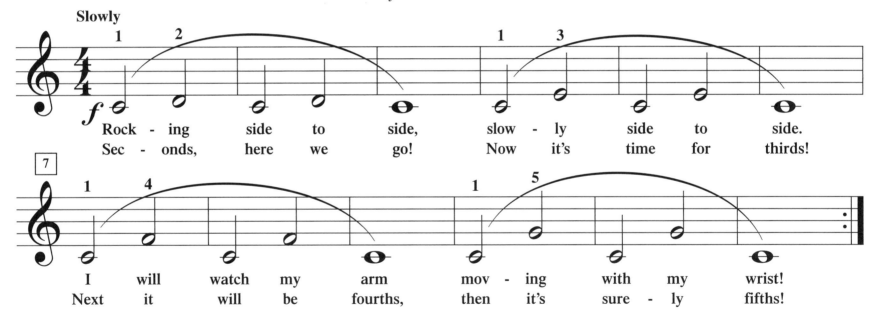

After playing, ask yourself:
- Did I play on the outside tip of my thumb?
- Did my arm and wrist rock side to side smoothly?

PLACE A ✓ UNDER EACH DAY YOU DO THIS TECHNIQUE.

MONDAY	TUESDAY	WEDNESDAY	THURSDAY	FRIDAY	SATURDAY	SUNDAY
____	____	____	____	____	____	____

FJH2051

Technique with Papa Haydn

Arm and wrist rotation

Rocking the Boat

by Helen Marlais

 CD 48 • MIDI 47

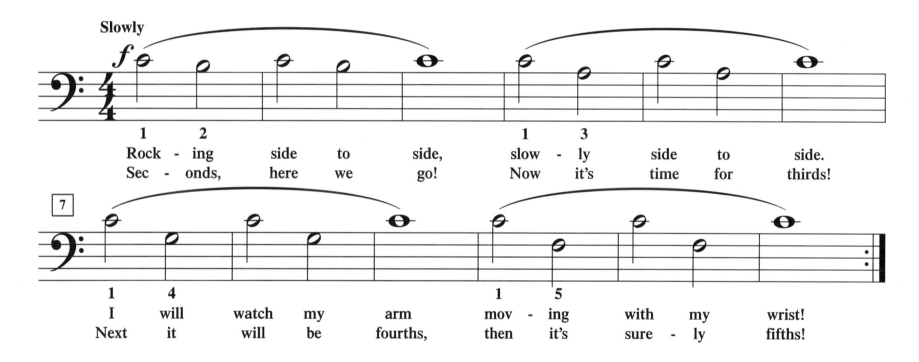

Slowly

1   2

Rock - ing   side   to   side,   slow - ly   side   to   side.
Sec - onds,   here   we   go!   Now   it's   time   for   thirds!

1   3

7

1   4

I   will   watch   my   arm   mov - ing   with   my   wrist!
Next   it   will   be   fourths,   then   it's   sure - ly   fifths!

1   5

After playing, ask yourself:
- Did I play on the outside tip of my thumb?
- Did my arm and wrist rock side to side smoothly?

PLACE A ✓ UNDER EACH DAY YOU DO THIS TECHNIQUE.

MONDAY	TUESDAY	WEDNESDAY	THURSDAY	FRIDAY	SATURDAY	SUNDAY
____	____	____	____	____	____	____

Before playing:

- Tap and count aloud the rhythm of the theme below.
- Which note will you start on? _____
- Which finger will you start on? _____
- Block (play together) the first 2 notes.
  Is this a 4th? yes   no (circle one)

Theme from Haydn's *Trumpet Concerto*

by Franz Joseph Haydn
1732-1809, Austria
Arranged by Kevin Olson

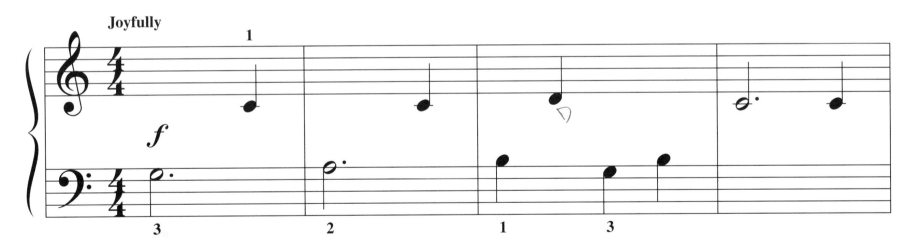

DUET PART: Kevin Olson (student plays 1 octave higher)

FJH2051

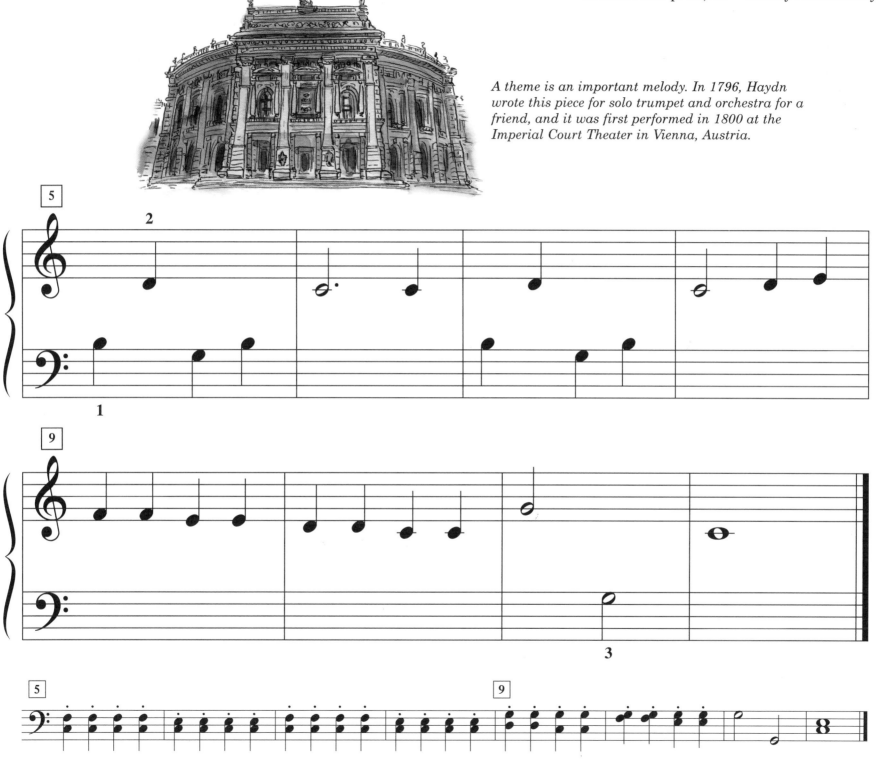

A theme is an important melody. In 1796, Haydn wrote this piece for solo trumpet and orchestra for a friend, and it was first performed in 1800 at the Imperial Court Theater in Vienna, Austria.

Learning Octaves

An **OCT**agon has _____ sides.
"OCT" is short for "eight."
The distance of eight notes
on the piano is an **OCT**ave.

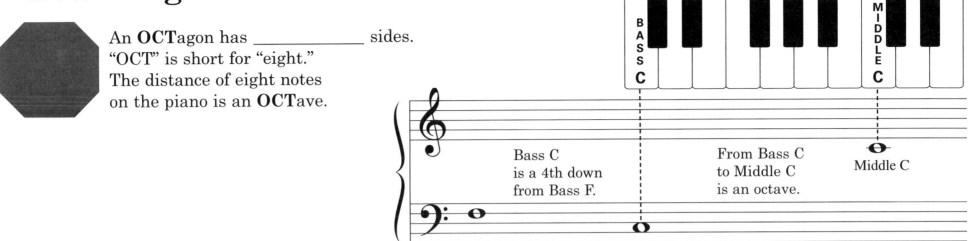

Bass F · Bass C

The Octave Song
by Helen Marlais

CD 50 • MIDI 49

With energy

Count all notes from C to C.

1 2 3 4   5 6 7 8!

Notes with the same name are an octave (8 notes) apart.
Can you count an octave in Spanish in the last 2 measures of the piece? *uno dos tres cuatro cinco seis siete ocho*

DUET PART: Kevin Olson

FJH2051

Technique with Papa Haydn

Weight transfer

 REVIEW THE TECHNIQUE ON PAGES 66 AND 67 AND ANY OTHER PAGES YOUR TEACHER ASSIGNS: _____.

- Transfer the weight of your arm from one finger to the next. Let your wrists roll in one smooth motion from one key to the next.

 **CD 51 • MIDI 50**

Clouds

by Helen Marlais

C Position

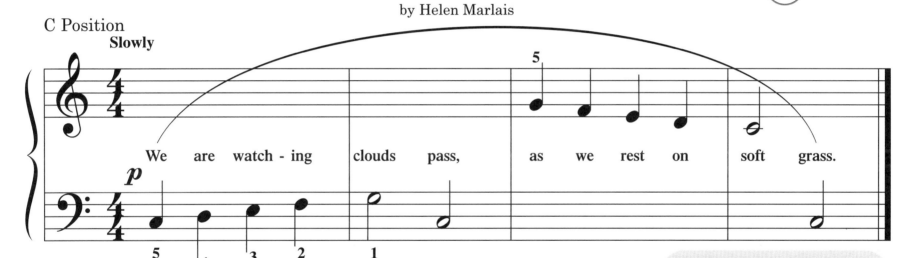

We are watch-ing clouds pass, as we rest on soft grass.

After playing, ask yourself:
- Where is the octave?

DUET PART: Timothy Brown (student plays 1 octave higher)

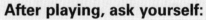

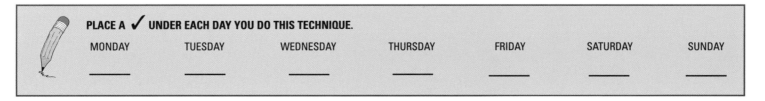

PLACE A ✔ UNDER EACH DAY YOU DO THIS TECHNIQUE.

MONDAY	TUESDAY	WEDNESDAY	THURSDAY	FRIDAY	SATURDAY	SUNDAY
___	___	___	___	___	___	___

Before playing:

- Find Bass F. The 1st note is a _____ down from Bass F.
- The letter name of the 1st note is _____.

 **CD 52 • MIDI 51**

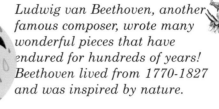

Ludwig van Beethoven, another famous composer, wrote many wonderful pieces that have endured for hundreds of years! Beethoven lived from 1770-1827 and was inspired by nature.

Cardinals in the Trees

by Helen Marlais

C Position

Brightly

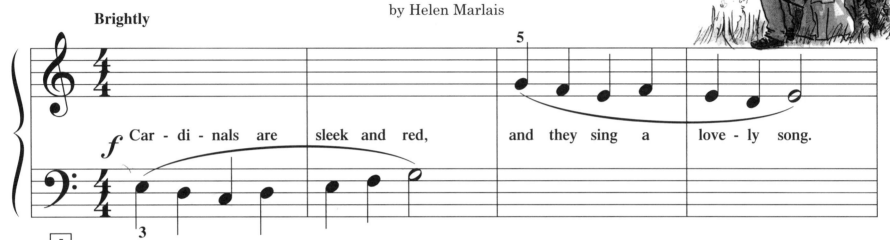

Car - di - nals are sleek and red, and they sing a love - ly song.

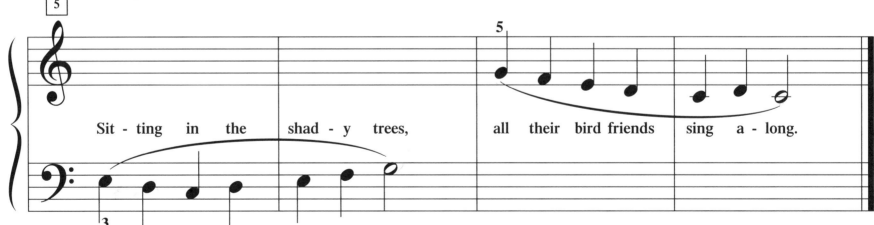

Sit - ting in the shad - y trees, all their bird friends sing a - long.

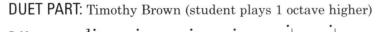 DUET PART: Timothy Brown (student plays 1 octave higher)

FJH2051

Before playing:

- Circle the only measure that is different in the 2nd phrase compared to the 1st phrase.

- Circle the repeated notes.

Now you can play one of Beethoven's most famous themes. A theme is an important melody. Beethoven wrote this theme as part of his "Ninth Symphony" which is for orchestra and chorus. The chorus sings about the friendship of all mankind.

Ode to Joy

by Ludwig van Beethoven
1770-1827, Germany
Arranged by Helen Marlais

CD 53 • MIDI 52

C Position

Andante

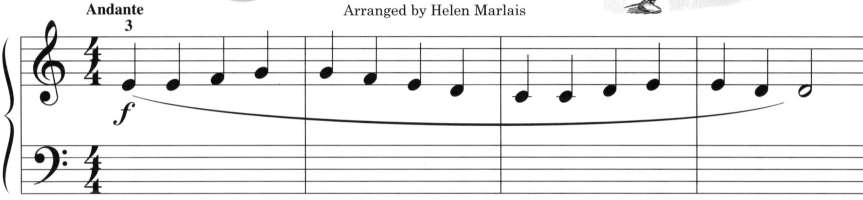

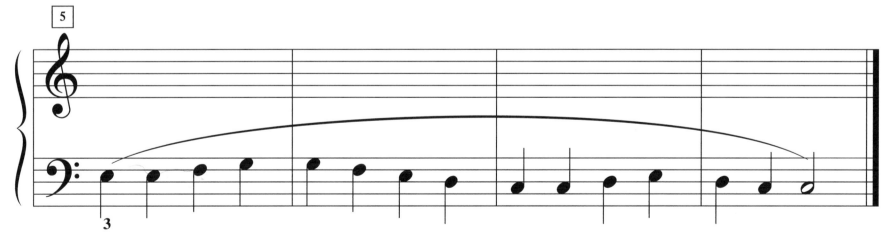

DUET PART: Timothy Brown (student plays 1 octave higher)

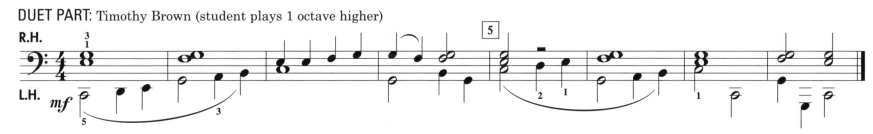

Before playing:

- Circle all of the Bass clef B's in *Haydn and Mozart*.
- Circle all of the 4ths. (There are 5!) Block these (play together).
- Can you find any 3rds?

Haydn and Mozart

Music by Johann Gottfried Walther
1684-1748, Germany
Lyrics by Helen Marlais

CD 54 • MIDI 53

Middle C Position

Hay - dn and Mo - zart, they lived long a - go, and they wrote their mu - sic

DUET PART: Timothy Brown (student plays 1 octave higher)

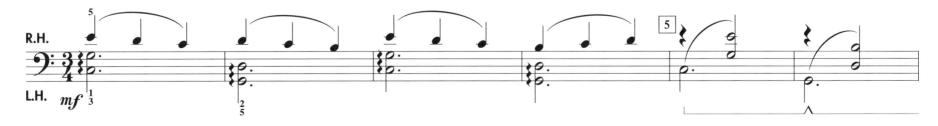

  FJH2051

Wolfgang Amadeus Mozart was born over 250 years ago. Like Haydn and Beethoven, Mozart was a musical genius who composed beautiful music and could play many instruments with ease. He toured Europe as a young boy. Mozart was born on Jan. 27, 1756, and lived until 1791. He lived only 35 years.

Tempo marking:

Moderato is an Italian word that means "at a medium speed."

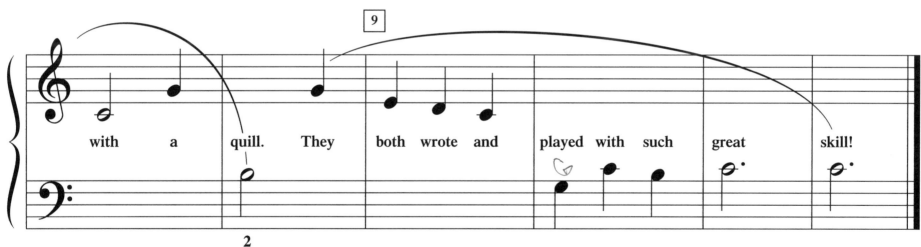

with   a   quill.   They   both wrote and   played with such   great   skill!

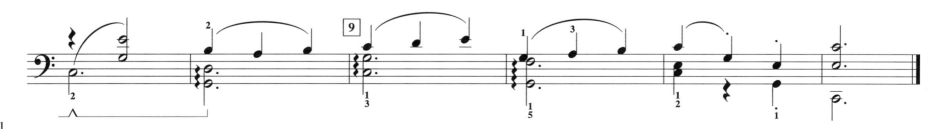

The Octave Sign (8va)

Before playing:

- Circle the 8va sign so that you will remember to move ~~~~

The 8va sign under the note in the L.H. means to play the note 1 ~~~~ er on the piano.

Dancing Raindrops

C Position

by Kevin Costley and Helen Marlais

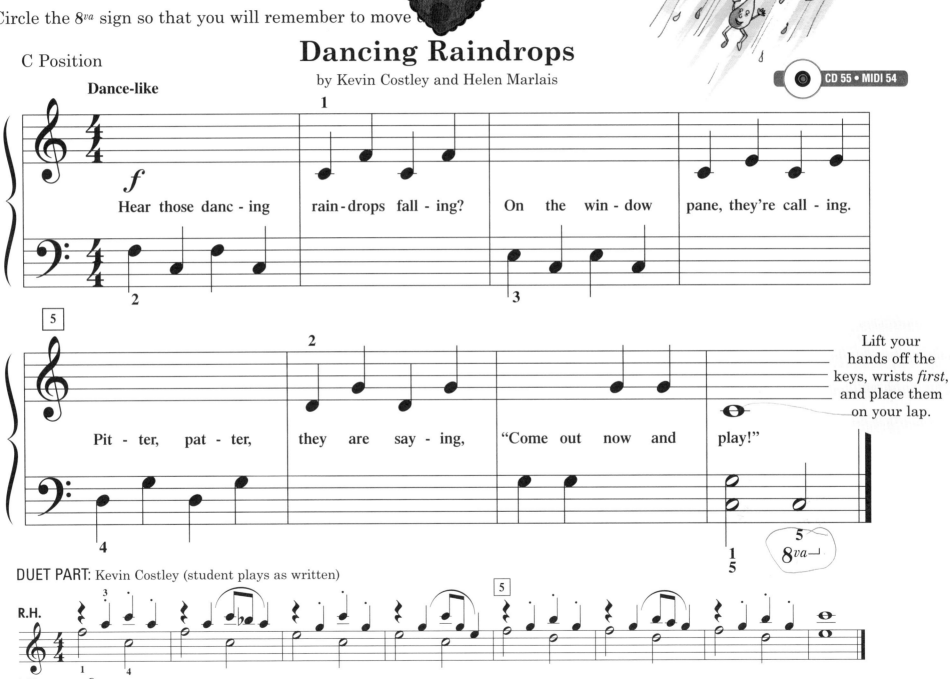

Dance-like

f

Hear those danc - ing | rain - drops fall - ing? | On the win - dow | pane, they're call - ing.

Pit - ter, pat - ter, | they are say - ing, | "Come out now and | play!"

Lift your hands off the keys, wrists *first*, and place them on your lap.

8va⌐

DUET PART: Kevin Costley (student plays as written)

R.H.

L.H. *mf*

76

FJH2051

Technique with Papa Haydn

Recital Book p. 39 · Theory and Activity Book p. 55, 56

"Drip-Drop-Roll" and Two-note slurs

- Drop your hand, wrist, and forearm straight down when you play the 1st note.
- On the 2nd note, roll your wrist towards the fallboard.
- Lift your wrist when you reach your fingertip.

> The *8va* sign above the note in the R.H. means to play the note 1 octave higher on the piano.

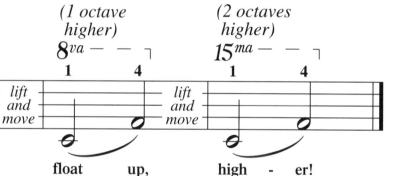

Floating Balloons

by Helen Marlais

CD 56 · MIDI 55

Bal - loons   float   up,   high - er!

Play the second note of the slur softer than the first note.

Now try the same technique with your left hand starting on a low C with finger 4.

Memorize *Floating Balloons* so that you can watch your hand shape and listen to the sound.

After playing, ask yourself:
- Did I play with a flexible wrist?
- Is the sound beautiful with the second note quieter than the first note?

PLACE A ✔ UNDER EACH DAY YOU DO THIS TECHNIQUE.

MONDAY	TUESDAY	WEDNESDAY	THURSDAY	FRIDAY	SATURDAY	SUNDAY
___	___	___	___	___	___	___

The Tie

> A tie is a curved line that connects two notes that are next to each other on the same line or space. It means to play the note only once, but hold it for the length of both notes!

Name the position:

___ Position

Candlelight Waltz

by Timothy Brown

CD 57 • MIDI 56

Gracefully

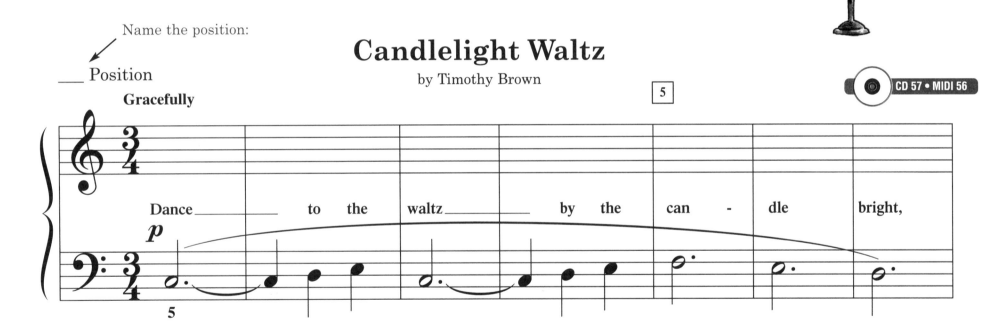

Dance____ to the waltz____ by the can - dle bright,

DUET PART: Timothy Brown (student plays 1 octave higher)

FJH2051

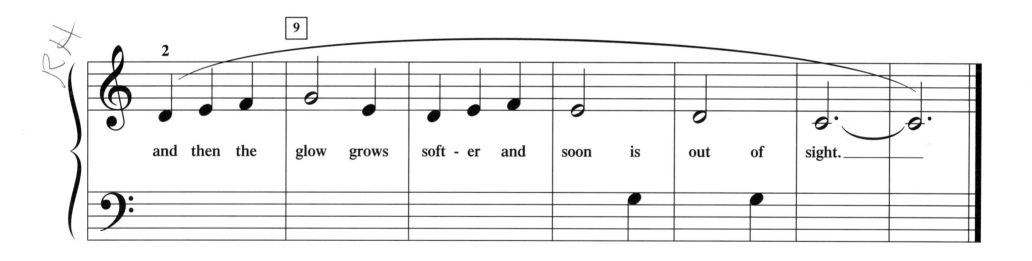

Before playing:

- Point to the notes and count aloud.
- Then point and speak the words.
- Block (play together) the 3rd in the L.H.
- Then block the 4th in the R.H.

When I Jump Out of Bed

by Mary Leaf

_____ Position

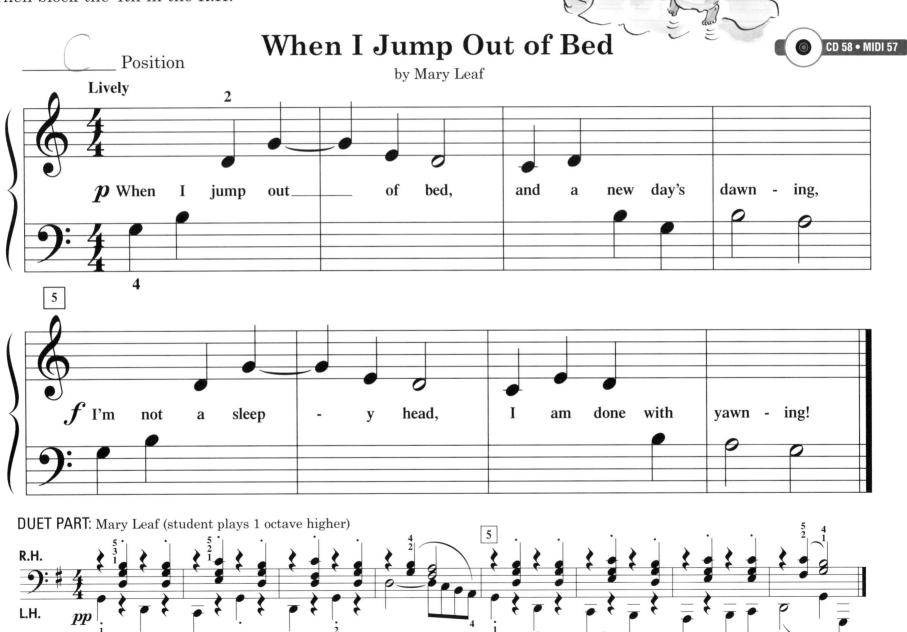

Lively

p When I jump out_____ of bed, and a new day's dawn - ing,

f I'm not a sleep - y head, I am done with yawn - ing!

DUET PART: Mary Leaf (student plays 1 octave higher)

R.H.

L.H. *pp*

FJH2051

Before playing:

- As you play low and high, shift your weight from side to side (left to right!)
- Feel your arm weight drop into the keys when playing 5ths.

Grand Entrance

by Helen Marlais

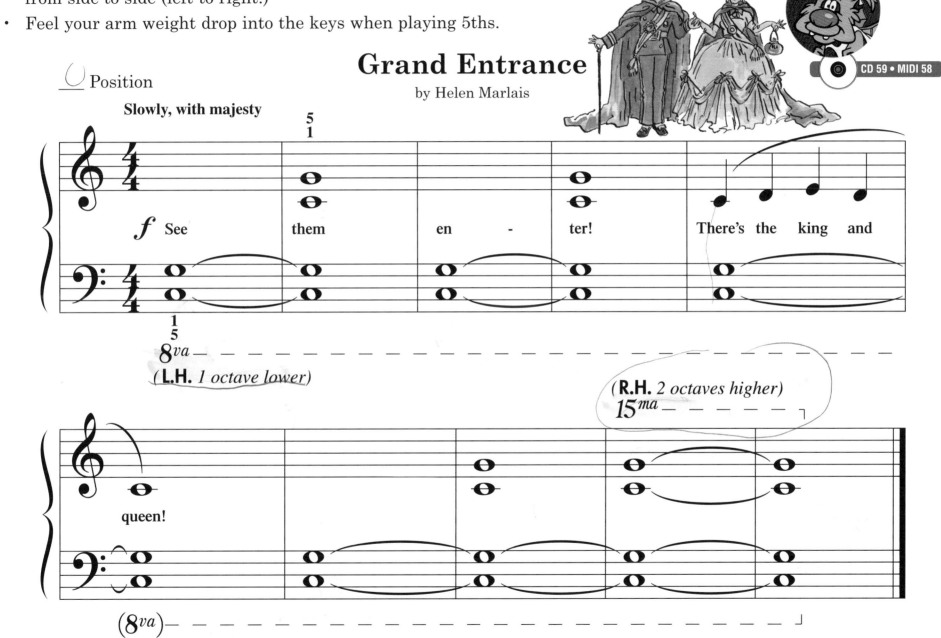

When you can play the piece, try using the damper pedal (the pedal on the right). Press down the pedal (heel on the floor) at the beginning of the piece and lift it when you lift your hands at the end.

Before playing:

- Point to the tied notes.
- Plan the 5ths in the L.H.
- Tap and count aloud.

Boat Song

(Barcarolle)

Music by Jacques Offenbach
Arranged by Timothy Brown
Lyrics by Helen Marlais

___ Position

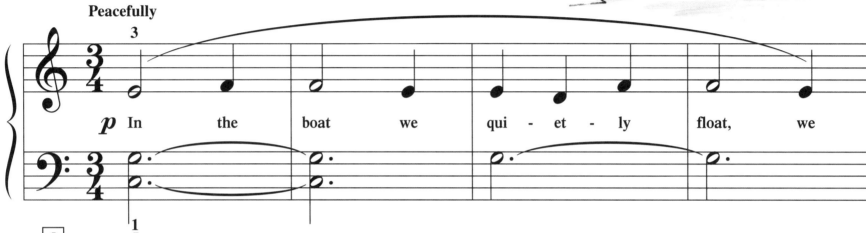

In the boat we qui - et - ly float, we

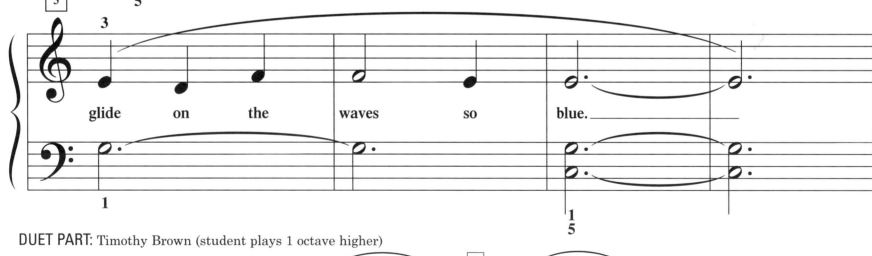

glide on the waves so blue.

DUET PART: Timothy Brown (student plays 1 octave higher)

FJH2051

Boat songs are typically written in 𝄴 time. Originally, boat songs, or "barcarolles" were sung by men who steered gondolas in Venice, Italy. Imagine that you are in Venice today with its more than 150 canals and 400 bridges! You could ride in a gondola through the many canals of this beautiful city.

Jacques Offenbach was a French conductor and cellist (1819-1880). He wrote many short operas that are light and cheerful. This melody is from one of his famous operas.

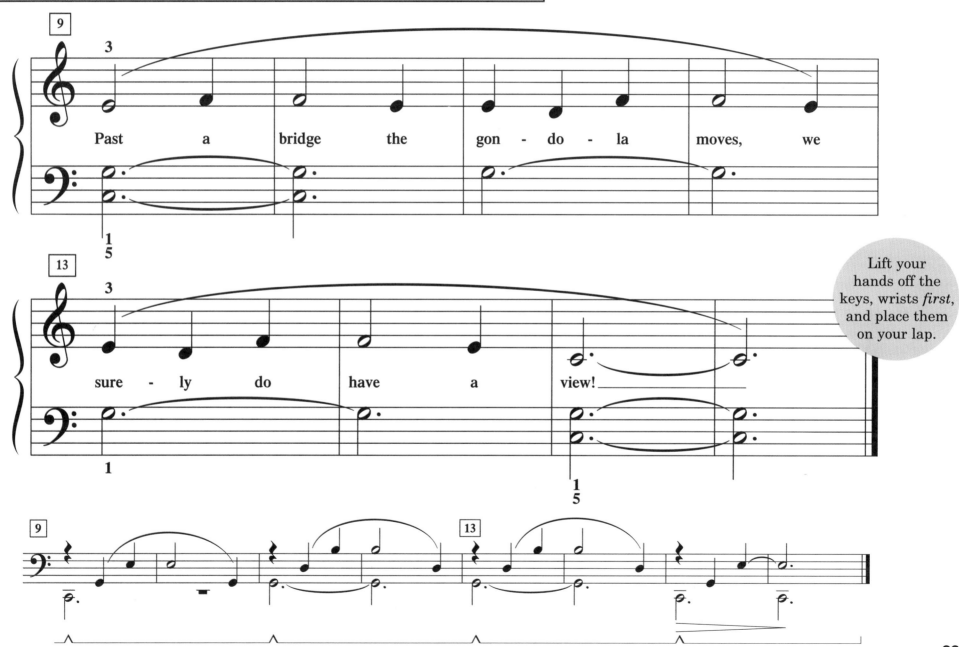

Past a bridge the gon - do - la moves, we sure - ly do have a view!

Lift your hands off the keys, *first*, and place them on your lap.

Before playing:

- Tap and count aloud.
- Say the letter name of each note in the Bass Clef.
- Find the octaves.

The County Fair Hoedown

by Kevin Olson

CD 61 • MIDI 60

Hear all the fid - dles play, all the town's here to - day!
Peo - ple all danc - ing 'round, oh, what a splen - did sound!

DUET PART: Kevin Olson (student plays 1 octave higher)

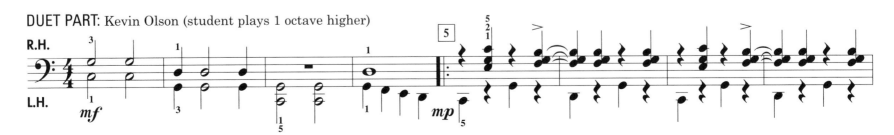

FJH2051

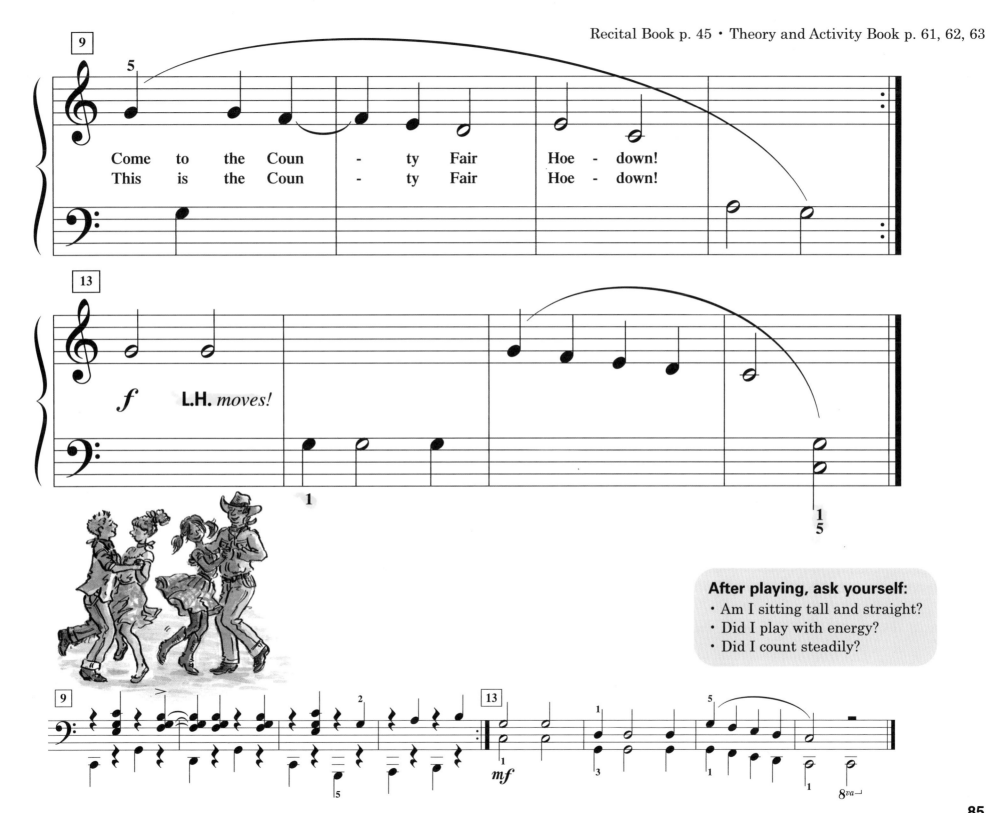

After playing, ask yourself:
- Am I sitting tall and straight?
- Did I play with energy?
- Did I count steadily?

Come to the Coun - ty Fair Hoe - down!
This is the Coun - ty Fair Fair Hoe - down!

f **L.H.** *moves!*

Music Dictionary

2nd (step):

3rd:

4th:

5th:

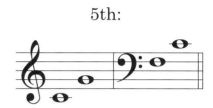

Music term	Definition	Found on page:
andante	an Italian word that means "walking" speed	.65
arm weight	how the arm should feel at the piano	.11
bass clef 𝄢	notes for the left hand are on this staff. It is also called the 'F' clef	.47
dotted half note 𝅗𝅥.	gets three beats	.44
double bar line ‖	shows the piece has ended	.12
dynamics	how loudly or softly to play, *forte* or *piano*	.29
forte (*f*)	an Italian word that means to play "loudly" or "strongly"	.26
half note 𝅗𝅥	gets two beats	.19
measure	a group of beats, separated by bar lines	.32
melody	a string of notes that make a tune you can sing along with or hum	.24

FJH2051

Certificate of Achievement

Emma
Student

has completed

Helen Marlais'
Succeeding at the Piano™

Lesson and Technique Book
PREPARATORY

You are now ready for
GRADE 1

T H E
F·J·H
MUSIC
COMPANY
I N C.

Frank J. Hackinson

April 11, 2021
Date

Michele Raul
Teacher's Signature